DEBATING THE STATE OF PHILOSOPHY

DEBATING THE STATE OF PHILOSOPHY

Habermas, Rorty, and Kołakowski

Edited by Józef Niżnik
and John T. Sanders

With contributions by Ernest Gellner and others

Published under the auspices of the Institute of Philosophy and Sociology of the Polish Academy of Sciences

Westport, Connecticut
London

Library of Congress Cataloging-in-Publication Data

Habermas, Jürgen.
Debating the state of philosophy : Habermas, Rorty, and Kołakowski / edited by Józef Niżnik and John T. Sanders.
p. cm.
"Published under the auspices of the Institute of Philosophy and Sociology of the Polish Academy of Sciences."
Includes bibliographical references (p.) and index.
ISBN 0–275–95715–2 (alk. paper).—ISBN 0–275–95835–3 (pbk.)
1. Philosophy, Modern—20th century—Congresses. 2. Philosophy—Forecasting—Congresses. I. Rorty, Richard. II. Kolakowski, Leszek. III. Niżnik, Józef. IV. Sanders, John T. V. Instytut Filozofii i Socjologii (Polska Akademia Nauk) VI. Title.
B804.H135 1996
101—dc20 96–20680

British Library Cataloguing in Publication Data is available.

Library of Congress Catalog Card Number: 96–20680
ISBN: 0–275–95715–2
0–275–95835–3 (pbk.)

First published in 1996

Praeger Publishers, 88 Post Road West, Westport, CT 06881
An imprint of Greenwood Publishing Group, Inc.

Printed in the United States of America

The paper used in this book complies with the Permanent Paper Standard issued by the National Information Standards Organization (Z39.48–1984).

10 9 8 7 6 5 4 3 2

In order to keep this title in print and available to the academic community, this edition was produced using digital reprint technology in a relatively short print run. This would not have been attainable using traditional methods. Although the cover has been changed from its original appearance, the text remains the same and all materials and methods used still conform to the highest book-making standards.

»» ««

Contents

»» ««

Preface

The pervasive feeling of dramatic change in the contemporary world has not left philosophy untouched. In a way characteristic of this discipline—namely, through manipulation of ideas and concepts—this feeling took the shape of a postmodern mode of thinking. One can reject the very idea of postmodernism or react to its texts with disgust (as many thinkers do), but such attitudes will not annihilate this intellectual fact (or anti-intellectual fact, as some would prefer to call it). Further, as has happened many times in the history of philosophy, both the "new" philosophical ideas and the vigorous opposition to them together create what we see as contemporary philosophy. Unlike in the past, however, it is becoming increasingly difficult to neglect the fact that even the most obscure ideas usually bear at least some relation to human life, whether explicitly or implicitly, and in some cases this relation may be quite rich in practical consequences.

The phrase "coping with contingencies" implies an effort to preserve or to regain an order within our world of ideas and to secure the coherence of a symbolic *universum*, the coherence of which is a primary need for every human being. As it happens, nothing can free philosophy from the task of reflecting on such efforts. Such tasks, moreover, can be seen as a confirmation of philosophy's identity and universality despite the many differences that appear in specific approaches.

The basic questions—albeit expressed in somewhat simplified form—underlying the differences among the contributors to this volume are the following:

1. Is our symbolic world a product of transcendent conditions, or is it rather a product first and foremost of our own capacities, notably our ability to use the conceptual and linguistic "box of tools" which we have at our disposal?
2. Can we argue for the special status of some of these tools—for example, our conceptions of 'the truth' or 'rationality'?
3. Are we prepared to give up our hunger for 'the Absolute'?

There is probably no better way to reflect on the contemporary status of philosophy than to confront the views of the most distinguished contemporary philosophers who have themselves placed their distinctive marks on its characteristics. There is, moreover, no better way to accomplish such a confrontation than to gather together such individuals and ask them to exchange their views in front of a professional audience. This is exactly what is presented in this book.

Jürgen Habermas and Richard Rorty met on May 8 and 9, 1995 in Warsaw. They had been invited to speak before the Institute of Philosophy and Sociology of the Polish Academy of Sciences, in order to discuss and debate their different perspectives on the contemporary state of philosophy. Originally, Leszek Kolakowski had been expected to participate as well, but a very unfortunate accident in Oxford just weeks before the event prevented him from coming. The text that Professor Kolakowski wrote for presentation on that occasion, however, along with the text of his subsequent written discussion with Professor Rorty, are included here. The late Ernest Gellner, along with a number of other excellent philosophers, joined the debate in due course. Professor Gellner's contributions, characteristically enough, were especially responsible for adding not only light but also a bit of welcome heat to the discussion.

In order to focus the whole debate on common topics, Professor Rorty proposed the following three questions which were agreed upon by Professors Habermas and Kolakowski:

1. Has the Enlightenment done more harm than good?
2. Can a secular culture produce enough of a civic community to protect democratic society against collapse?
3. Is the notion of "rationality" of any use in articulating the nature of such a secular culture?

There is no doubt that these questions created a basic framework for all of the contributions and for the subsequent discussion. What is especially interesting is that, without exception, the dominant concepts and problems that appeared in the texts of all three main participants were those of relativism and rationality. Everyone agrees, of course, that there are no final solutions to these problems. But the debate shows—in a fascinating way—that these problems create what are probably the most important philosophical issues of contemporary human life and constitute the core of contemporary intellectual anxieties. The debate shows also that there is no more important thing to do, academically speaking, than to be aware of these problems and that there is no better path to this awareness than through philosophizing.

Because of severe time constraints, Professor Habermas was unable to do the necessary editing of his spontaneous oral contributions to the later parts of the discussion. These contributions are therefore not included in the present volume.[1] But he had written his original contribution with the text of Professor Rorty's contribution before him, and it seems to us that he has managed to bring his own position on the issues under discussion into as clear a light as he has ever done previously, especially as regards the contrast of his position with that of Professor Rorty.

The debate marked the fortieth anniversary of the foundation of the Institute of Philosophy and Sociology of the Polish Academy of Sciences. The Institute, founded in 1956, managed to preserve genuine philosophical study during the dark years of communism. The celebratory debate was possible thanks to the generous help of Jürgen Habermas and Richard Rorty, who kindly agreed to meet in Warsaw and then to edit their texts. The book which resulted from this meeting was made possible, in turn, by the work of a number of my colleagues from the Institute who helped in changing the recorded words into a written form. In addition, I must express my sincere gratitude to Dr. David Gellner, who edited both of his late father's contributions to the debate. Finally, I owe special thanks to Jack Sanders, who helped me in editing the volume at a time when such help was of utmost need.

Józef Niznik

NOTE

1. The Foundation of The Institute of Philosophy and Sociology (ul. Nowy Swiat 72, 00–330 Warsaw; fax [48 22] 26 78 23) can supply (with the full permission of all participants) a set of three video tapes featuring most of the debate.

Chapter 1

Coping with Contingencies

JÜRGEN HABERMAS: COPING WITH CONTINGENCIES— THE RETURN OF HISTORICISM

One way to deal with the rather unspecific topic of the "present state of philosophy" is to focus on an obvious feature of contemporary debates—the contextualist mood that prevails in most of the debates, whether in moral and political philosophy, the philosophy of language, or the philosophy of science. This orientation reminds me of that style of *Historismus* that began to dominate German philosophy in the late nineteenth century. It was not until after World War II that historicism[1] was superseded by more systematic, mainly phenomenological and analytical approaches. Starting with Dilthey's *Lebensphilosophie* and leading up to Rorty's neopragmatism, I am going to compare certain features of both, the old and the new kind of historicism.[2]

Loyal to Rorty's spirit I will try to do this in narrative rather than strictly argumentative terms.[3] Let me first use the guiding question "How to cope with contingencies?" as a general scheme of interpretation for the history of philosophy at large and develop the dialectical pattern of Platonism, anti-Platonism, and anti–anti-Platonism (I). Wilhelm Dilthey's approach will then serve as the model for an analysis of what Ernst Troeltsch has called *Das Problem des Historismus*—the question of historicism (II). Martin Heidegger's response to this impasse in *Being and*

Time paved the way for a kind of linguistic contextualism that led, on a different level of reflection, to a renewal of historicism (III). I will conclude my introduction to this debate with some remarks on Richard Rorty's neopragmatism, which I regard as the most sophisticated version of present historicism (IV).

I. The Dialectics of Anti-Platonism

Following Dewey's "quest for certainty," one might look at the history of philosophical idealism as a sequence of attempts to come to terms with ever new kinds and categories of perceived contingencies, be they the forces of mythical powers, the processes of a demythologized nature, or the events of an objectivated history. Following a rather conventional interpretation of the origins of Greek philosophy, the invention of Logos and *theoria* served to overcome the contingencies of a world that had been interpreted in terms of mythical narratives. Let me (1) sketch the move toward Platonism, (2) explain the double nature of the response which the move got from its critics, and (3) apply this dialectical pattern to the present debate.

First, observed from the angle of psychohistory, the transition "from myth to logos" appears as a parallel development of the emerging world religions founded at about the same time by great prophetic figures. From this perspective, Socrates appears side by side with Buddha, Confucius, Moses, and Jesus Christ, followed by Mohammed later on.[4] The break with mythical traditions that Buddhism, Confucianism, Hinduism, and the monotheistic religions achieved in the dimension of existential and moral reasoning, philosophy accomplished within the cognitive dimension. On both sides conceptual frames emerged, which allowed the human mind to occupy a transcending point of view, one located either beneath or beyond the world. In our tradition we still speak of a "God's Eye View." This phrase only exemplifies a more general phenomenon: With their transcendent perspectives, believers and philosophers alike gained an unprecedented distance from the world as a whole.

Under the encompassing gaze of believers and philosophers, 'the' world gains contours different from the horizon of 'our' lived-in world. The world now can be objectivated from either a theoretical or a moral point of view—as a totality of entities or sociomoral relations. Both philosophy and religion learned how to distinguish the eternal and infinite from the transitional and finite; they "discovered" immovable substances and ideas that persist through the passing flows of appearances. The regime of arbitrary mythical powers was dismantled as soon as the world was split up into surface phenomena and essences. This explains, in the case of metaphysics, why the idealist emancipation of theory from praxis was supposed to have a liberating effect. The Platonist construction of an eternal world of ideas behind the phenomena was linked to a theoretical attitude and, moreover, to a philosophical life of contemplation, which was perceived, no less than the religious life-patterns of the monk or the hermit, as a curriculum for catharsis and salvation. Here, reason and theory served as means to free the human mind from the threatening contingencies of a mythical world. It was, of course, only from hindsight that mythical powers could appear as irrational forces.

The reverse side of this emancipation through theory was the perception of a new kind of dependency brought about by rationality itself. The Logos of human speech and thought now appeared as a mere reflection of and being subordinated to the eternal Logos of an ideal order of things. From a critical point of view, the regime of arbitrary mythical powers only had been replaced by a regime of necessary and timeless universals. Reason owed its capacity to cope with the bizarre contingencies of an obsessed and bewitched universe to the very achievement of abstraction. Persisting universals had been dug out from fleeting particulars, the permanent from the temporal, necessary and law-like forms from accidental events. For the suspicious eyes of critics, the new regime of reason stood out as even more inexorable than the old one, especially against the background of those promises of enlightenment that had accompanied philosophical reasoning from the start. The successful dissolution of the deceptions of a mythical world and the satisfying experience of getting rid of its bewildering arbitrariness made philosophers all the more sensitive of the price they had to pay in terms of another dependence—dependence on rational constraints from an ideal order of essences. The dialectical replacement of fateful contingencies by logical necessities was felt as an odd irony from early on; this disappointment nourished an anti-Platonist distrust in the authority of abstract universals that emerged as early as Platonism itself. The critical countermove was to reveal what Platonism had buried under the cover of its false abstractions.

Second, the anti-Platonist philosophers carefully, and scornfully, traced the marginalized, repressed, concealed, and forgotten features of the 'non-identical,' the particular and the transient that had been absorbed in the constructs of abstract universals. Anti-Platonists denounced an idealism which hypostatizes its own constructions as something 'given' or 'found'. They ironically insisted on the emancipatory effect of unleashing the repressed contingencies from the fetters of an ideal world that first had been invented with the very same emancipatory intention. In the course from Platonism to anti-Platonism, 'the contingent' changes places: While the eternal world of ideas once was supposed to cope with contingencies, now the promise of liberation shall be fulfilled by facing hidden contingencies pulled from behind the veil of illusory ideas.

But irony catches up with this second move as well. The anti-Platonist destruction of abstract universals only led to a nominalist conceptualization of the world which acknowledged the contingencies of a profane and de-essentialized nature. And with the release of this new kind of natural contingency, nominalism again stimulated the very desire idealism had met before—namely, the desire not only to face critically unravelled contingencies, but to cope with them. For this purpose the critic once more had to employ the very reason he or she had so efficiently denounced for false abstraction earlier. To be sure, reason had in the meantime lost its metaphysical innocence. The anti-Platonists are now aware of reasons's own contributions to the construction of what only appeared as the order of things. A disquieting process of self-reflection had transformed contemplation into a critique, suspicious of and sensitive to its own illusions. At the same time, it has become more and more obvious that self-critique itself is a double-edged process. The practice of criticizing Platonist pseudo-objects moves within a conceptual frame and employs conceptual means which cannot in turn be deconstructed without depriving anti-Platonism of its own critical sting. The radical attempt to do away with any abstraction, idealization, or concept of truth, knowledge, and reality that transcends the local *hic et nunc* would run into performative self-contradictions.

One cannot reduce all universals to particulars, all kinds of transcendence to immanence, the unconditional to the conditional, and so on, without presupposing these same distinctions and tacitly making use of them.

Third, a reading of the history of philosophy that focuses on the funny to-and-fro movements of Platonism and anti-Platonism provides good reason for opting out of the game and finishing it once and for all. The question is whether Richard Rorty can do so without merely starting the next round of the same game.

From the repetitious cycles of an enduring dialectics of enlightenment we learn that today's anti-Platonism has a heritage as impressive as Platonism itself. The anti-Platonist spirit emerges from important materialist, sophist, and skeptic strands in classical Greece. This critical attitude even seizes power with late medieval nominalism and extends via early modern empiricism (still prevailing in the Anglo-Saxon world) and throughout the nineteenth century up to Nietzsche, American pragmatism, and German historicism. These movements share a critical attitude toward metaphysics and a liberal one in politics. Each of them equally responds to a new wave of perceived contingencies. Whether anti-Platonist motivations arose from the broader social processes of urbanization and commercialization, mobilization of resources and manpower, or modernization in general, the philosophical background was always the perception of complex phenomena which spilled over the boundaries of established interpretational schemes. These irregularities, at first channeled as mere anomalies, finally burst the received conceptual patterns, convicting them of the idealist fallacy of overgeneralization or false abstraction. As we have seen, the anti-Platonist critique usually proceeds in two steps. First, the deconstruction of hypostatizations is intended to do justice to formerly repressed contingencies; the next and more inconspicuous move toward a new scheme of interpretation is meant to offer instruction in how to cope differently with this new kind of contingency.

The great paradigm shifts from ontology to mentalism and, again, from subject-centered to linguistic philosophy follow from this type of deconstructive and reconstructive response. Broadly understood, they are inspired by the nominalist assumptions of classical empiricism and historicism/pragmatism, respectively. New philosophical paradigms have to cope with perceived contingencies—not just with new kinds of contingencies felt in everyday life, but with contingencies of an objectivated nature and history that are perceived through the lenses of new types of sciences, such as modern physics in the seventeenth century and the *Geisteswissenschaften* in the nineteenth century. In both these cases, philosophy had to react to new kinds of contingencies set aflow and legitimated by science and research. Empiricism took the shape of an epistemology of the natural sciences and historicism that of a methodology of the human sciences (or *Geisteswissenschaften*). Yet the representatives of these important, paradigm-generating anti-Platonisms soon became targets of another criticism. Their opponents point out inconsistences in the hidden presuppositions of the successful anti-Platonist critique. Kant's transcendental critique of Hume's interpretation of causality is the best known example. I will move immediately to another example of this anti–anti-Platonist strategy, namely, to Heidegger's transcendental-ontological critique of Dilthey's historicist account of reason. Those figures complete the cycle of a relentless critique by proving the concealed reconstructive nature of what appeared as a straightforward deconstruction of idealist abstractions.

While I am in political sympathy with the anti-Platonist iconoclasts, my philosophical sympathy is on the side of the custodians of reason in those periods when a justified critique of reason loses the awareness of the implications of its inevitable self-referentiality, as with Aristotle, Thomas, Kant, and (even) early Heidegger (once understood in this way).

II. The Problem of Historicism

The rise of historical consciousness in the late eighteenth century is reflected in a whole set of concepts clustering around "history" in the singular. As Reinhard Koselleck has shown, "the" history, including all aspects of human life, takes the place of those many histories in the plural. Until the eighteenth century, history had served as a repository for exemplary stories which supposedly can tell us something about the recurring features of human affairs and thus feed the anthropological curiosity for patterns of human behavior. Once the focus of attention shifts, however, from the exemplary to the individual, from the typical to the unique, from returning cycles to unknown futures, from continuities to ruptures and changes, from similarities to differences, history gained a completely different meaning and relevance. History—in terms of an experienced instead of a physically measured stretch of time—advanced into the primary medium for individuation. Persons are individuated through their life-history, and cultures and cultural forms of life are individuated through historical periods or epochs. It is no surprise that this historical consciousness gave birth to an evermore intense awareness of evermore widely spreading contingencies. This explains the need to cope with a kind of contingency which no longer emerged from the core of outer or inner nature but arose from the surface of fluid human affairs, interpersonal relations, and social networks.

Since Aristotle, history had always been conceived as the paradigmatic sphere of the contingent, the transitory, and the particular. But for exactly this reason it had remained beyond philosophical interest and outside of science proper—a realm of mere empirical interest, off limits to *episteme*. It was not until the end of the eighteenth century that history also became a domain of theoretical interest and research. The rise of the *Geisteswissenschaften* posed a challenge to the metaphysical division of labor between *theoria*, designed for the knowledge of the necessary, timeless, and universal, on the one hand, and empirical or common-sense knowledge on the other. The humanities took off from a *Verwissenschaftlichung der Menschenkenntnis* (K. Ott).

Among the leading philosophers of the time, Hegel was the first who vividly felt the threat posed by the spreading of historical contingencies to grand theory. He realized that even truth itself is drawn into the flux of time—"die Wahrheit fällt in die Zeit." Accordingly, Theodor W. Adorno has coined the phrase "Zeitkern der Wahrheit." I will pass by those failed attempts to extend the strong concept of "theory" to the domain of history. There is no philosophy of history, pretending to discover patterns of reason in the changes of history, that was not soon torn apart by historical research. This explains, by the way, the hostility of the German Historical School toward Hegel, whom Ranke and all the others perceived as an authoritarian *maître de penseur*. By the end of the nineteenth century, the humanities had been so successful that philosophy had not only lost sovereignty over their territory but was forced to receive its own basic categories from the humanities: Sign and sentence and language and communication provided the frame for the linguistic turn; action and symbolic interaction and praxis and production inspired pragmatism; the lived-in body in its natural habitat and the socialized self became cues for philosophical anthropology; and a historicist *Lebensphilosophie* focused on culture and the cultural forms of life and on history and the historical mode of being. In fact, all of these new approaches had a historicist ring and sprang from a similar motive. That form of historicism, which came full circle only with Derrida and Rorty, in fact started one hundred years ago.

At that time, the humanities had piled up overwhelming evidence for the contextual nature of reason, truth, and knowledge and of the works of the human mind in general. Only the media of this contextualization—language and action, culture and history—were left as candidates for the philosophical analysis of "infrastructures." The last Platonic residues could easily be exorcised in the merciless light of historical ruptures, peculiarities, and differences. If any structural features were left at all, the invariants would be revealed only in the heart of the life of history itself. In this situation, Wilhelm Dilthey took a rather conventional start with his intention to develop a methodology of the human sciences in the more or less Kantian fashion of a "Critique of Historical Reason." In the end he came up, though, with something quite different—a philosophical hermeneutics which was supposed to discover the structural core of historical life.

Let me first summarize Dilthey's expressivist model of interpretation and then discuss the difficulty that became known as the "problem of historicism."

First, the perception of (the qualities of) an object provides the classical model for an epistemological analysis. Dilthey replaced this model by a new one: the reading of a text. Interpretation was the primary method of the humanities anyway. Historians, linguists, and social scientists get access to their cultural object-domains not by observation but by understanding symbolic meanings. The interpretation of a written source is exemplary for the approach to cultural objects of all kinds—from sentences, actions, and gestures (via persons and their biographies) to mentalities, styles, and traditions, and finally to cultures and societies, including their political institutions, economic systems and so on. For all these phenomena Dilthey coined the term *Lebenszusammenhänge*—forms or contexts of life. Unlike Husserl, who conceived the life-world as constituted by a transcendental subject, Dilthey appropriated Hegel's notion of the objective spirit in his own way; he conceived cultural forms of any kind as 'objectivations'. It is by symbolic 'objectivations' that 'subjects' 'express' their 'experience'. Let me explain how Dilthey understood these terms.

'Objectivations' are of a symbolic nature, like signs, which provide the material substratum for an immaterial meaning—whether a document proves the authorship of an important political decision, a letter reveals a particular character trait of a person, or a chair exemplifies the style of a cultural period. More difficult is the term 'experience' (*Erlebnis*), the content of which gets objectivated. Dilthey appeals to an expressivist idea; for example, the manifestation of an emotion of anger or anxiety in mimetic reactions, gestures, or other somatic symptoms. Though hermeneutics is by no means restricted to these phenomena, the expression of a psychological state or episode in body language serves as an analogue for the meaning-conferring role of an 'experience'. Most difficult to explain is the 'subject' to whom we attribute such an experience. Again, the paradigm is the individual person, expressing her or his mental states in utterances of whatever kind: in speech or action, in habits or products, or in the art-work of a life-history (Foucault, too, is not only a critic but at the same time, however unconsciously, a follower of Dilthey). The paradigm case of the author of a biography (Dilthey himself has written quite a few famous biographies) is extended to units and communities of any scope: peoples, states, societies, cultures, epochs, and so on. It is important to keep in mind that all these 'subjects', be they individual or collective actors, participate in the joint venture of an encompassing historical life.

The three terms—objectivation, experience, and subject—finally form the context for an implicit definition of the term that is constitutive of the expressivist model: A subject 'expresses' an experience in terms of an objectivation. With this conceptual frame Dilthey develops, from an analysis of interpretation, a structural model of historical life. His basic assumption is that interpretation, both in its scientific and in its everyday mode, is an essential feature of historical life. The 'objectivated' meaning is the result of an act of externalization, while the original 'experience', expressed as symbolic meaning, is in turn transformed through an act of internalization into a kind of reenacted experience or *Verstehen*. Historical life is like breathing meanings out and in:

	Externalization		*Internalization*	
Leben:	Erleben —	Ausdruck	Verstehen —	Nacherleben
	(experience)	(expression)	(interpretation)	(reenactment)

The act of interpreting an objectivated experience is identified as just one step in the sequence of an encompassing process of historical life. Interpretation terminates in understanding, that is, in the reenactment of the original experience, by which the interpreter expands the horizon of his or her own experience and starts another cycle of externalization and internalization.

The holistic nature of historical life, in which all human beings, alive or dead, are involved, explains furthermore the circular movement of interpretation. Any single act of interpretation is guided by an intuitive preunderstanding of the shared whole of life, while this anticipation is in turn checked and revised by the explicit understanding of the particular feature under investigation. This "hermeneutic circle" does not, however, reflect only the methodology of the historical sciences, but the ontology of the life of history as such. It does not just explain the professional performance of the historian, but the historical mode of existence of human beings in general. Historians only raise to the level of an expert's knowledge what is constitutive for the accomplishments of everyday life. In our daily wheelings and dealings we cannot but keep moving in the life-circle of the externalization and internalization of meanings.

Second, the problem with such an approach is, briefly, an implicit naturalization of truth and reason. While entangled in the ups and downs of the historical life cycles, in both their pretheoretical and scientific mode, interpreters lose the very distance from their object-domain that is necessary for discriminating between true and false or correct and incorrect interpretations. If the act of interpretation is part and parcel of that historical life which at the same time is turned into an object of interpretation, any standard for a critical evaluation must be taken from within a context that puts interpretation on a par with the interpreted phenomena.

In order to avoid a naturalist fallacy, Dilthey was at first inclined to defend an objectivist theory of *Verstehen*. He took interpretation as an analogue of observation. Both seem to reproduce some "x"—either an object, which causes an adequate perception through sensory stimulation, or a subjective experience which confers meaning on the (understood) symbolic expression. As the perception presents an image of the object, interpretation presents a kind of image of the original experience. But again, this realist interpretation of interpretation fails to account for an uneasy implication of the holistic nature of the historical process, in which interpreters find themselves "always already" involved. Unlike an observer, the interpreter is a participant who, like a speaker in front of an audience, has to take a performative attitude toward second persons. The interpreter can no longer assume a third-person, objectivating perspective which is supposed to be somehow outside the object-domain and clearly distinct from the phenomena in need of interpretation. As Hans-Georg Gadamer has explained, the interpreter would not understand anything if he or she were not located within a process in which both the interpreter and his or her object are embedded from the start. Since there is no way out of this context for the interpreter, his or her interpretation is no less a manifestation of historical life than the interpretandum is. This applies as well to the standards by which interpretations can be critically evaluated. If there is any such standard at all, it must be inherent in historical life.

In his own work Dilthey employs aesthetic standards that are congenial to his expressivist model of interpretation. A subject can express his or her experience more or less vividly, deeply, richly, sincerely, or authentically; in like manner, the interpretation can be better or worse depending on the vitality, depth, richness, or authenticity of the reenactment of the original experience. Interpretations can be deep or shallow, but not true or false. Manifestations display the same grammatical features as expressive speech acts—they are linked to claims of sincerity, truthfulness, or authenticity, but not to truth-claims.

If authenticity is the only available standard for critical evaluation, Dilthey has to face an uneasy consequence, first and foremost, for the epistemic status of truth-claiming enterprises like religions or metaphysical worldviews, moral belief systems, philosophies, and theories in general. Conceived as 'manifestations' of historical life, they can only be judged as more or less authentic expressions of authors or underlying mentalities, styles, cultures, forms of life, and so on. But the same holds also for historical interpretations of those phenomena. Humanist accounts, too, appear as more or less authentic documents of the interpreter's capacity to empathetically appropriate those original experiences embodied in the objectivations he investigates. This obviously has a self-referential implication for any philosophy which, like Dilthey's, claims to provide higher-order interpretations. The assimilation of all meaningful objects to manifestations of something subjective poisons the cognitive status of Dilthey's own philosophy.

This problem became obvious when Dilthey presented his famous typology of philosophical worldviews. The tripartite classification of naturalism and subjective and objective idealism is presented as a scheme that allows one to describe any philosophy as an objectivation of one of three fundamental or existential orientations, but it does not allow questions about the truth or falsity of any of these approaches. If one supposes that this typology is inclusive and that there is no standard for evaluating the truth of these conflicting types, a similar indeterminacy of theory choice would apply to the typology itself—and to the philosophy, of which the typology forms a part. Depending on the place interpreters happen to occupy in historical life, there must be many different typologies of the same kind—*Weltanschauungstypologien* (as, in fact, there were). In general, if there is no validity claim besides the context-dependent claim to authenticity, the enterprise of interpretation as a whole cannot count as a serious candidate for the promotion of knowledge and learning, not to mention science (in the sense Dilthey still understood the *Geisteswissenschaften*, including philosophy).

III. A New Kind of Historicism—and Three Responses

Historicism sprang from a methodological self-reflection within the *Geisteswissenschaften*. In retrospect, Dilthey's historicism does not appear as a position particularly strong in its philosophical premises. But in Germany, where Kant never ceased to have a deep impact, the challenge of historicism provoked a move toward what is now called "detranscendentalization." The growing awareness that the contingencies of history had gained philosophical relevance increasingly undermined the extramundane status of an ahistorical and disembodied transcendental subject. Whatever previously had been conceived as accomplishments of pure transcendental reason, Dilthey and his students found "always already" situated and embodied within some historical form of cultural life. They therefore faced the task of reconciling the world-constituting faculty of the transcendental subject with the innerworldly features of a symbolically localized reason. Interpretation, the via regia of the humanities—not speech and action, as in the case of American pragmatism—was the key for solving this problem. The *Geisteswissenschaften* had shaped German academic culture. Here, Hamann and Humboldt, Schleiermacher, and the hermeneutic tradition in general had shown the path towards detranscendentalization from early on. Heidegger moved further in this direction and reached, beyond Dilthey, a point where his conclusions unexpectedly overlapped with those of the later Wittgenstein. In spite of different backgrounds and rather opposite styles of reasoning, the convergence of Heidegger's and Wittgenstein's approaches at least became obvious for the following generation, which set the stakes for the present debate on rationality.

Far from any philological ambition, I will confine my loose remarks first to Heidegger's critical move beyond Dilthey and second to three contemporary reactions which are typical for the new kind of historicism.

First, read as a response to Dilthey, Heidegger's *Being and Time* points to a way out of the cul-de-sac of a self-refuting relativism. The expressivist model was still rooted in the philosophy of the subject, which Heidegger overcomes by introducing a contextualist concept of "the world" (which is similar to the pragmatist world-concept of Peirce and Dewey, though focused on disclosure rather than problem solving). Heidegger conceives the world no longer as the totality of facts or entities, but as the lived-in social space and historical time that form the horizons of our everyday practices. The expressivist model still reckoned with some individual or collective subject manifesting feelings, desires, beliefs, and so on. Terms like 'subjective experience' and 'objectivation' as well as the quasi-organic rhythm of 'externalization' and 'internalization' (of breathing out and in) still betray the epistemological design of subject–object relations. Heidegger, who hated the term *Erlebnis* and the expressivist approach as such, replaces subjectivity with *Dasein*. He slips the human being from all subjectivist connotations, defining *Dasein* in purely functional terms. *Dasein*—being-in-the-world—is explained in terms of the structure of which it is a function. Dilthey's *Lebenzusammenhänge* are turned into the networks of *Bewandtnis- und Bedeutungszusammenhänge*. While world disclosure is wedded to the transcendental spontaneity of what formerly had been conceived as 'constituting' the world of objects, the semantic fabric of a lived-in world is now 'disclosed' by a prevailing language.

This linguistic turn was possible because Heidegger received and kept one important insight from Dilthey: For him, too, interpretation does not count as a special kind of activity but is rather constitutive for the very mode of how human beings perform and lead their lives (*"Verstehen als Grundzug des Daseins"*). As human beings, they find themselves within a world that is 'preinterpreted' in the sense that it illuminates and, at the same time, structures an *a priori* understanding of anything people may encounter and must cope with in their world. Heidegger decouples interpretation from the reenactment of experience. Symbolic meanings no longer depend on the objectivation of subjective experience. They are, instead, rooted in language and stand on their own grammatical feet. That the limits of our language are the limits of our world is as true for Heidegger as for Wittgenstein. A language is conceived as the repertoire of enabling conditions for interpreting whatever may occur to members of the speech community within the bounds of their world. The semantic range for possible descriptions also determines the horizon for practical encounters with all possible occurrences in the world. Heidegger thus directs our attention to the holistic preunderstanding of a meaningfully articulated world, the ontology of which is inscribed in the grammar of a world-disclosing language.

The move from Dilthey's expressivist model to Humboldt's transcendental conception of world disclosure allows Heidegger both to keep interpretation and understanding in the center of an ontology of historical life and to give this ontology a linguistic turn (even if he himself became aware of this implication only afterward). In a nutshell, a shared language is constitutive for a 'world'

- that provides a context-forming frame of implicit meanings
- which at the same time establish possible relations in which language-users find themselves embedded
- when they, in their practical encounters, happen to face some "x" within the world
- and with which they can only cope by interpreting and understanding this "x" as fitting under some type of description
- while drawing from the stock of their ontological preunderstanding of the world.

By relating interpretation to grammatical and, more generally, to symbolic structures rather than subjective experiences, Heidegger gains the resources necessary for solving the problem of historicism. While Dilthey had narrowly confined interpretation to the manifestations of some underlying subjectivity, Heidegger extends the scope of interpretation beyond expressions of self-representation and authenticity to the whole set of semantic contents and validity claims. He can save meaning and validity and the related concepts of reason, truth, and knowledge from getting naturalized because he retains Husserl's transcendental distinction between *constituens* and *constitutum* in terms of the ontological difference between a linguistically disclosed world and entities in the world.

Heidegger, moreover, attributes to philosophy the extraordinary role of administering those ontological categories that rule culture and society in each epoch. The intuitive preunderstanding of a world shared by ordinary people is explained by the metaphysical theories of the time. The history of metaphysics can thus gain a sublime authority incomparable with anything else (except for poetry). Contemporary philosophy, in any case, faces the eminent task of a self-reflexive examination of the history of metaphysics. The deconstruction of a sweeping Platonism that, since the original step from myth to Logos, seized hold of occidental rationalism will now result in a metahistory of ontological frames, including Nietzsche's self-confessed anti-Platonism. Transcending the conceptual limits of metaphysics from within is a preparatory exercise for the paradoxical reversal of the metaphysical way of thinking—"*vom verfügenden Denken zum Andenken des Seins.*"

Second, let me (from my reading of Heidegger) extrapolate those two assumptions that, as far as I can see, mark the base lines for the present debate on rationality:

- The deconstruction of the Platonist heritage allows us to discover a plurality, if not a sequence, of world-disclosing languages, ontologies, discourses, vocabularies, power regimes, traditions, and so on, each of which occupies a specific place in social space and historical time.
- These ontogrammatical regimes are inclusive in the sense that they (1) provide a semantic network for how any possible encounter with something in the world would fit specific descriptions and (2) settle standards according to which possible interpretations or interventions could be evaluated as true or successful.

This is an oversimplified picture, but it covers an argument which has provoked an enduring debate. Let me mention three typical responses.

First, some of those who take the inclusive nature of world-disclosing languages for granted defend the descriptive thesis of a pluralism of mutually incommensurable worldviews. They assume that each ontogrammatical regime defines, for its domain, different conditions of truth and efficiency, thereby manifesting a rationality of its own, while all of these rationalities enjoy an equal standing. Without going into details, it is hard to see how one could maintain such a position and at the same time avoid the well-analyzed problems of either a self-defeating relativism (Feyerabend) or a "happy positivism" (Foucault).

Second, among those who share the assumption of the inclusive nature of world-disclosing languages, others accept Gadamer's critique of hermeneutic objectivism, Davidson's critique of a conceptual scheme, or both. They abandon the thesis of incommensurability (at least in the strong sense of an incommensurabilty of validity and meaning). Depending on whether or not they remain faithful to the hermeneutic model, they part company in different directions. The hermeneutic model requires from participants in dialogue the mutual presupposition of symmetrical relations between "us" and "them." But each, deconstruction and assimilationism, struggles with difficulties of its own.

Deconstructionists join Heidegger in his belief that philosophy (in a division of labor with poetry) holds a privileged place as a custodian of being. The history of metaphysics is expected to reveal the fateful traces of subsequent epochs of a Platonist—that is, a distorting—world disclosure. In accordance with the contextualist premise of hermeneutics, this history of metaphysics can be grasped only from within the horizon of metaphysics itself. We would, however, not fully understand the fate of Platonism unless we could liberate ourselves, at least partly, from the grammatical spell and the specific selectivity of this tradition. Though starting from within the inescapable horizon of Platonism, we must at the same time try to transcend it and turn the tools from this conceptual universe critically against themselves. As a consequence, the "overcoming of metaphysics" remains a self-confessedly paradoxical enterprise.

Assimilationists abandon the hermeneutic maxim that every interpreter is bound to symmetrical relations between communicating parties, both of which reciprocally grant the possibility of learning from each other. Interpretation is no longer understood as an accomplishment of mutual understanding but as a self-related enterprise which, instead of coming to terms with others, at best promotes the expansion of one's own horizon or ends up with surrender to a superior tradition. On this premise, the communication between members of competing and mutually exclusive traditions may reach the point of an "epistemological crisis," where assimilation of or conversion to the standards of the other side is the only choice left (MacIntyre).

Third, Richard Rorty's methodological "ethnocentrism" is a somewhat different conclusion from the same assimilationist model of interpretation. Rorty appropriates Heidegger's goal of "overcoming metaphysics" in a deflationist attitude. He shares the idealist faith in the privileged position—and world-historical impact—of philosophy only in retrospect, while arriving at a much more sober conclusion for the present. Rorty simply recommends that we opt out of the whole game of Platonist and anti-Platonist moves. In coping with their self-generated contingencies and risks, modern societies would fare better without any philosophy. We are admonished to get rid of the dualisms we owe to the Platonist heritage and to give up misleading metaphysical distinctions between knowledge and opinion, between what is and what appears as real or legitimate. We are told to emancipate our culture from the philosophical vocabulary clustering around reason, truth, and knowledge. Compared with postmodern elitism, this pragmatic demand for replacing the inherited vocabulary with a new, less deceiving and more illuminating one promises a more radical and more consistent version of contextualism and gives Rorty a unique place in the present discussion.

According to Rorty's conception, the world-disclosing function has become reflexive. We are now aware of how our vocabularies serve the creative function of letting us see situations and problems in a different—and one hopes a more convenient—useful, and efficient way. It is up to us language-using animals to produce new and better vocabularies in a similar way as we have always produced new and better tools. Compared with the high tone of the Heideggerians, the neopragmatist concern with problem-solving activities has the liberating effect of bringing agency back from the heaven of an obscure metahistory of being to the earth of ordinary people who must cope with the problems of their world.

IV. Some Critical Remarks on Neopragmatism

Does Rorty succeed in finishing with the philosophical language game as such? While pretending to do so, he seems only to start another round of the same game. If this observation is correct, the assumption about the inclusive nature of world-disclosing languages, the founding premise of antifoundationalism, is up for reconsideration.

My brief critical remarks will relate (1) to the paradoxical features of the naturalist version of an "overcoming of metaphysics" that neopragmatism inherits from its idealist counterpart; (2) to some well-known difficulties of all naturalizing redescriptions of truth and knowledge; and (3) to an unconvincing replacement of empirical and moral knowledge by ethical self-understanding.

First, I could not agree more with Rorty's statement that "various contemporary contributors to the pragmatist tradition are not much inclined to insist either on the distinctive nature of philosophy or on the preeminent place of philosophy within culture as a whole."[5] While giving up the elitist self-understanding of philosophy, Rorty retains the deconstructionist premise that we still live under the ontogrammatical spell of a pervasive metaphysical language. Rorty parts company with Heidegger and Derrida in his deflationist program. He criticizes the Platonist tradition no longer from within, but wants to finish it via the fiat of a new vocabulary. This has interesting implications.

At first, Rorty translates the paradoxical nature of deconstruction into the frank performance of double talk. For people like me, who supposedly still suffer from metaphysics, Rorty intends his talk to be understood in the conventional way as a flow of good and convincing arguments; colleagues should be beaten with their own weapons. Those others, however, who have already been converted to neopragmatism will no longer mistake Rorty's utterances as truth-vehicles or expressions of veridical beliefs; they will recognize them as rhetorical devices for influencing people's beliefs and attitudes. Under a description that renders questions of truth and rationality meaningless, 'persuasion' just helps people to get socialized in a new language. So far, so good. But Rorty could only manage to accomplish all of this by deploying an alternative—which in fact turns out to be a new—vocabulary.

Since Rorty dispenses with the paradoxical intricacies of playful deconstruction, the language he introduces in a straightforward manner for purposes of reeducation cannot benefit from the surplus value of a self-critique of metaphysics. The new language does not enjoy the peculiar legitimation of being the result of the deconstruction of an old and illusionary one. Its legitimacy depends on nothing but expediency. The new vocabulary is supposed to better fit the present conditions of life.

If we look at it more closely, the new language appears, however, neither new nor particularly functional. The conceptual frame which Rorty introduces for "coping" and "problem solving" is well known from nineteenth-century naturalism, when people like Spencer extended the Darwinian conception of mutation, selection, and adaptation from the field of biology to the social and cultural sciences (without much success, by the way). The language game of the survival of the fittest may at best count as one among several more or less established vocabularies, so that we need reasons why we should prefer this one. Even if Rorty could base his preference on the presumed scientific success of the neo-Darwinist approach to evolution, there would remain a necessity to justify, in general, the exemplary authority of science. This kind of scientism would need some supporting philosophical argument. If philosophy, literature, science, and politics do not form different genres but provide as many tools for coping with changing environments, as Rorty assures us, scientific success would, however, stand as just one among several criteria for legitimating new vocabularies.

Rorty might object that a new vocabulary does not need any legitimation besides reproductive fitness or functional success. But this criterion would work against neopragmatism. Rorty admits that the so-called metaphysical distinctions "have become part of Western common sense."[6] This being an indicator of the efficient functioning of that Platonist vocabulary, we lack a good reason for giving it up. The functional fit of Platonism with present circumstances provides sufficient legitimation for continuing that language game. On this premise one cannot understand why Rorty's own enterprise of overcoming metaphysics should satisfy any need at all (as Tom McCarthy has argued).

Second, philosophically more interesting is Rorty's attempt to adapt the practice of argumentation to a description that would fit the Darwinist frame. He deprives claims to truth and validity of any idealizing connotation—of bursting provincial boundaries and transcending local contexts—and redescribes truth as usefulness. In levelling the epistemological distinctions between 'making' and 'finding,' 'constructing' and 'discovering,' 'programming' and 'convincing,' between what appears as true to us and what is true, Rorty again steers the course of deflationism. I agree with his penetrating criticism of realist conceptions of "truth as correspondence," and I also accept the Deweyan proposal to explain "truth as warranted assertability." But Rorty himself points to a difficulty arising from what he calls the "cautionary use" of the truth predicate ("p" is well justified, but it still might not be true).

This grammatical feature is not only an indicator of our fallibilism, but reminds us that we must not confuse the parochial meaning of "'p' is rationally acceptable in the given context of justification" with the decontextualized meaning of "'p' is rationally acceptable" (which is to say, "true in general, not just in this local context and by our present standards").

The problem with any epistemic conception of truth is how to draw and maintain this clear-cut meaning difference without falling back into some sort of Platonism (or realism). Can we do justice to the undeniable moment of unconditionality that we, by the forceless force of grammatical rules, in fact link with the use of the truth-predicate, without taking recourse to any kind of idealization? If 'truth' is explained in terms of rational acceptability, and if the cautionary use of the truth-predicate reminds us of the fact that what is 'justified' by our best available standards might still not be 'true', we must not assimilate truth to rational acceptability. We have to build some reservation into the notion of rational acceptability if we want to bridge the gap, but we must not blur the line between '-is true' and '-is justifiably held to be true'. We must stretch the referent of the idea that a proposition is rationally acceptable 'for us' beyond the limits and the standards of any local community. We must expand the universe of 'all of us' beyond the social and intellectual boundaries of an accidental bunch of people who just happen to gather under our skies. 'True' would otherwise merge with 'justified in the present context'.

This is the reason why Rorty, in his discussion with Hilary Putnam, was step by step pushed to imbue the critical auditorium, which authorizes rational acceptability, with ever stronger connotations. In order to avoid the confusion of truth with justifiability, the process of justification must meet demanding requirements. If somebody states "that p," he or she must (implicitly at least) be prepared to justify "p" by appealing to a rationally motivated agreement of other publics, not just ours, a public of experts, an ever wider public of reasonable persons, or a public of people who are "better versions of ourselves."

Rorty even specifies the conditions for the required context of free and tolerant discussions. While granting equal access to all relevant persons, information, and reasons, this form of communication should rule out any kind of exclusionary and repressive mechanisms, propaganda, brainwashing, and so on. In stressing the open, inclusive, nonrepressive features of a communication within a more and more idealized auditorium, Rorty approaches willy nilly my description of "rational discourse" and Putnam's formula of truth as "rational acceptability under idealized conditions." With this kind of "superassertability," Rorty unintentionally slides, however, back into the domain of what he calls a "Platonist culture."

Third, there remains a plausible reason and an honest motivation for distrust in idealizations. The (supposedly misleading) belief that we should approach, in both theoretical and moral reasoning, a *focus imaginarius*—a true picture of reality or a moral point of view—would divert us, Rorty fears, from the practical goal of simply attaining more satisfaction. By contrast, the promotion of well-being requires us to assimilate truth and moral rightness to happiness. Rorty therefore identifies the conditions for making beliefs 'true' and behavioral expectations 'right' with those conditions that make them "conducive to human happiness." He simply stipulates what meaningful reasoning is all about. An ethical type of reasoning—in the Aristotelian sense of deliberating about what is good for me (or for us) in the long run—displaces all other kinds of reasoning. Even if Rorty could explain why we should substitute, from a first-person perspective, ethical reasoning for empirical and moral judgment, it is hard to see how the assimilation of truth to happiness could at all be implemented in scientific as well as daily practices.

The displacement of third- and second-person reasoning by first-person reasoning also explains the neopragmatist critique of realism in epistemology and cognitivism in moral theory. As far as (internal) realism is concerned, Rorty criticizes the presupposition of an objective world that imposes certain constraints on descriptions of what happens in the world. Let me mention that this purely formal presupposition is just as compatible with an epistemic notion of truth as with the indissoluble interpenetration of language and reality—the linguistic mediation of any contact with it. Far from restoring the "myth of the given," it only keeps 'objectivity' apart from 'intersubjectivity' and saves the about-relation of propositions (to something in the objective world) from collapsing with the interpersonal relations among those who check a proposition's truth (within the horizon of a shared life-world). Otherwise, conflicting theories would no longer offer themselves for a comparative evaluation in terms of their being 'true' or 'false' or 'better' or 'worse'. This is the conventional picture Rorty wants to change.

If conflicting theories are well confirmed within their respective contexts, they should not be taken as competing but as different theories. They cannot compete for anything but the satisfaction of context-depending needs. 'Good' theories fit the needs at certain times and places; if they keep fitting they will adapt to different times and places. In support of this thesis Rorty offers the following example: "When we say that our ancestors believed, falsely, that the sun went around the earth . . . we are saying that we have a better tool [for satisfying our needs]. . . . Our ancestors might rejoin that their tool enabled them to believe in the literal truth of the Christian Scriptures, whereas ours does not. Our reply has to be . . . that the benefits of modern astronomy and of space travel outweigh the advantages of Christian fundamentalism."[7] I think the example works in the opposite direction. I, at least, could easily do without the man in the moon and imagine that I would prefer, if I could choose by the standards of William James, a belief in God the *salvator*. What speaks against the assimilation of truth to happiness is simply the fact that there is no choice. The grammatical fact that believing is different from choosing seems to express a feature of the human condition rather than a superficial trait of a linguistic convention or a tradition that we might change at will.

A similar consideration holds for the proposed assimilation of 'I am obliged to . . . ' to 'it is good for me. . . '. There are so many examples of the painful difference between 'what is just' and 'what is advisable for me (or us)', that I cannot see how one could conflate one with the other and still explain why we should follow the very maxims Rorty rightly suggests, maxims of "Diminish human suffering and increasing human equality."[8] By pragmatic standards, these are indeed excessive demands. How could we convince people to implement these maxims in general practices if we could only appeal to the promotion of each one's happiness, instead of finding out, from a moral point of view, the right thing to do? The moral point of view requires us to perform another idealization, namely to imagine you and me as members of the inclusive community of human beings and to strive for the role of a fallible, yet impartial, judge on what would be equally good for everybody.

I have tried to take the Kantian role of an anti–anti-Platonist, who seriously accepts the critical part of his nominalist, empiricist, or contextualist opponents, but still tries to convince them (in the traditional way) that they are not sufficiently critical of the remaining elements of idealization in the tacit presuppositions of their own striking arguments. This leads me to recommend setting aside the misleading idea about the inclusive nature of world-disclosing languages.

According to this idea, a linguistically disclosed world *a priori* fixes the rules of what counts as true or false and rational or irrational for 'us'—members of the corresponding speech-community—who are locked into this particular world as long as the ontogrammatical regime of the language happens to last. This radical contextualism relies on the proposition that meaning determines validity but not vice versa. I would propose, instead, that the interaction between world disclosure and innerworldly learning processes works in a symmetrical way. Linguistic knowledge and world-knowledge interpenetrate. While one enables the acquisition of the other, world-knowledge may, in turn, correct linguistic knowledge (as Putnam convincingly argues). Relevant parts of a world-disclosing language that first enables speakers and actors to look at, cope with, and interpret in a specific way anything that might occur to them can well be revised in the light of what they have learned from their innerworldly encounters. There is a feedback between these results of learning processes and those linguistic conditions which make this learning possible in the first place. This repercussion is owed to the context-transcending range and context-bursting force of criticizable claims to validity on the intersubjective—but fallible—recognition on which our daily communicative practices depend.

RICHARD RORTY: EMANCIPATING OUR CULTURE

I am very grateful to Professor Niznik and his colleagues for this opportunity to discuss the similarities and differences between my own views and those of Professor Habermas. I find Habermas's historically oriented paper very rich and stimulating. It made me rethink not only the relation between Dilthey and Heidegger but the shape of the last century of philosophical thought.

As you know, Napoleon said that he did not care who wrote a nation's laws if he could write its songs. It seems to me that one need not care who writes the philosophical systems if one can write the history of those systems. Narratives of the history of philosophy are among the most powerful tools of persuasion which we philosophers have at our disposal. Among all of Habermas's books, the one I admire most is *The Philosophical Discourse of Modernity*, for it seems to me the most complete and plausible retelling of the story of recent philosophy presently available. So I shall try to sketch an alternative narrative of the last few centuries of philosophy, putting the emphases at different places than those at which Habermas puts them.

I entirely agree with his suggestion that the Platonists' construction of an eternal world of ideas behind the apparent world of daily life was no less a project of salvation and catharsis than was the religious life-plan of the monk or the hermit. In the West at least, the figure of the knower, a figure which Plato pretty much invented, has been the dominant form of spiritual life for the intellectuals. To end Platonism one needs to offer an alternative form of spiritual heroism. As I see it, the struggle between the Platonists and the anti-Platonists is a struggle between the form of spiritual perfection which Plato described and a new, romantic, humanistic, secular form.

I take the common denominator of secularism and romanticism to be Protagoras's claim that man is the measure of all things. This claim was restated in the works of the British Romantics, particularly in Shelley's *Defense of Poetry*. Shelley there says that the poet's function is to glimpse the gigantic shadows that futurity casts upon the present. Shelley's point was that instead of looking for the influence of the eternal on the temporal, or the unconditioned on the contingent, we should just forget about the relation between eternity and time. We should concentrate on the relation between the human present and the human future. I take Shelley to have been restating Protagoras's point—or what may, at any rate, have been Protagoras's point—that there is nothing outside of human beings that provides guidance to human beings. I take Protagoras to have suggested that human beings are on their own.

If one takes the alternative to Platonism to be this romantic version of secularism, then one will have a story to tell about the history of recent philosophy which is rather different from Habermas's. I tell a story which is specifically American and is, perhaps, an example of our famous American cultural imperialism. On my (only half-serious, highly chauvinist) account, the founder of recent philosophy was Ralph Waldo Emerson. Emerson restated the Protagorean thesis that human beings are on their own—that their own imagination will have to do what they had hoped the gods, or a scientific knowledge of the intrinsic nature of reality, might do.

Nietzsche carried Emerson's writings in his knapsack when tramping the Alps in the summertime. William James knew Emerson as a friend of his family's. Dewey called Emerson "the philosopher of democracy." Emerson can be seen as having initiated two traditions of twentieth-century philosophical thought. One is European, starting from Nietzsche and going on through Heidegger to Derrida. The other is the American pragmatist tradition, which runs from James to Dewey to Quine to Davidson.

I can illustrate the spirit of what I am calling secularism and romanticism by telling a story about Emerson Hall at Harvard. Emerson Hall is the building in which the Philosophy Department works. When it was built, at the end of the last century, the Harvard Philosophy Department was asked what the inscription on the facade should be. William James persuaded the department that the inscription should be Protagoras's motto: "Man is the measure of all things." Then James and his colleagues went off to spend the summer in Europe, pleased with their decision. But when they came back in September they found that the inscription read "What is man that thou art mindful of him?" This was because President Eliot of Harvard was neither a secularist nor a romantic. Eliot did not want the philosophers to go public with their Protagoreanism.

On the historical account I would offer, the central struggle between twentieth-century quasi-Platonists and their Protagorean/Emersonian opponents is the latter's attempt to replace the search for universal validity with utopian social hope. Plato, and Greek philosophical thought generally, took our ability to *know*, and more specifically to know nonhuman reality, as the crucial human potentiality. The pragmatists want to put social hope in the place that knowledge has traditionally occupied.

The American pragmatists are not the only Emersonians to make this attempt. Consider Derrida's recent work. Derrida nowadays puts a great deal of emphasis on what he calls "the only undeconstructable notion," namely, the messianic hope for justice. If you think of Derrida as the culmination of European Emersonianism, you will think of him saying something like this: "If we stop thinking of truth as the name of the thing that gives human life its meaning, and stop agreeing with Plato that the search for truth is the central human activity, then we can replace the search for truth with the messianic hope of justice."

I think of this Derridean initiative as cohering with Hume's naturalistic criticism of epistemological rationalism, and also with the criticisms made by John Stuart Mill and William James of the Kantian notion of unconditional moral obligation. These two lines of criticism are aimed at the two great themes of Platonic thought, the two great forms of the demand for unconditionality—a kind of unconditionality which can come only from something eternal and not from something human, historical, and contingent. The first line of criticism is aimed at the idea of an unconditional demand for absolute truth and at the attempt to attain, outside of mathematics, the apodicticity associated with mathematical truth (the attempt in which Husserl thought philosophy must persist in order to be true to itself). The second is aimed at the Kantian notion of an unconditional moral law. I see Humean naturalism and pragmatism, as well as certain trends in post-Nietzschean European philosophy, as emphasizing the contingent character of both attempts at cognition and attempts to achieve moral responsibility.

If you accept these criticisms of the Platonic demand for unconditionality, then you may agree with me that if you have democratic politics, as well as artistic and literary freedom, you do not need to think much about truth, knowledge, and *Wissenschaft*. Instead of thinking of the center of human life as the worship of the gods, as it was before Plato, or as the search for truth, as it has been throughout the Platonic tradition, you can think of the center of human life as democratic politics and art—each mutually supporting the other, and impossible without the other.

So, when Habermas says that I am advocating a view according to which we should emancipate our culture from the whole philosophical vocabulary clustering around reason, truth, and knowledge, this seems to me exactly right. It is not that there is anything wrong with reason, truth, and knowledge. All that is wrong is the Platonic attempt to put them in the center of culture, in the center of our sense of what it is to be a human being. I think of the naturalism of Dewey and Davidson on the one hand and the romantic idealism of Derrida on the other as complementing one another (as one would expect from two Emersonians) and giving us an alternative to Platonism.

To put all this another way, I should like us to detach the notion of rationality from that of truth. I want to define rationality as the habit of attaining our ends by persuasion rather than force. As I see it, the opposition between rationality and irrationality is simply the opposition between words and blows. To analyze what it is for human beings to be rational is (and here I take up a familiar theme from Habermas's own work) to understand techniques of persuasion, patterns of justification, and forms of communication. There is, it seems to me, considerable convergence between Habermas's substitution of communicative reason for subject-centered reason and what I am calling the Protagorean/Emersonian tradition.

The principal differences between Habermas and myself concern the notion of universal validity. I think that we can get along without that notion and still have a sufficiently rich notion of rationality. We can keep all that was good in Platonism even after we drop the notion of universal validity. Habermas thinks that we still need to keep it. But compared to the similarities between my Emersonian secularist romanticism and his notion of rationality as the search for undistorted communication rather than as an attempt to get from appearance to reality, this difference may not be so very important.

Professor Habermas has mentioned his astonishment at Whitman's ability to take for granted the possibility of poetic, spiritual progress within an industrialized society.[9] This sort of optimism about industrial societies is often thought to be peculiarly American, so there may be an interesting America–Europe contrast here. Yet it is worth noting that in Derrida's mind the contrast is not America versus Europe, but Jew versus Greek. For him, the messianic hope of justice is specifically Jewish, as opposed to the Greek search for the logos, the Platonic ideal of knowledge.

But this is just a passing remark. The only real point I want to make in response to Professor Habermas's remarks concerns the question of how to reply to religious fundamentalists. I think it is quite true that in my country fundamentalism is gaining strength, and I attribute this to diminished economic opportunity. I think the traditional alternative to religious fundamentalism in America has been a romantic version of Americanism—a romance common to Whitman, Franklin Delano Roosevelt, and Martin Luther King, Jr. We Americans have usually been able to rely on a patriotic civic religion, centering around the Whitmanesque romance of democratic vistas, rather than upon the Kantian triplicity of spheres of culture, when we need an answer to religious fundamentalists. This traditional strategy is not, I must admit, working very well these days.

The Jeffersonian compromise—trading a guarantee of religious freedom for the willingness of religious believers not to bring religion into discussion of political questions—has been a very important part of American national life. If this compromise ceases to be taken for granted, then we American romantic secularists may well, in the relatively near future, find ourselves at the mercy of the fundamentalists. If fascism comes to America, it will be in association with fundamentalism.

I confess that if I had to bet which country would go fascist next, my bet might be on the United States. This is because we Americans are suffering the consequences of the globalization of the labor market, without having established a welfare state. So we are much more vulnerable to right-wing populism than are most European countries. But if one asks what the intellectual's response to this vulnerability should be, my bet would still be on this romantic religion of the nation—the religion of which Whitman, Roosevelt, and King are prophets.

NOTES

1. *Historismus* is the label for the philosophical and methodological background assumptions of the representatives of the *Deutsche Historische Schule*. The English term "historicism" which I will use in the text is ambiguous. As with K. R. Popper, it often relates to a philosophy of history that assumes a "logic"—or specific "laws"—of history. But the *Deutsche Historische Schule* stood in straight opposition to exactly this Hegelian heritage.

2. *Neohistorismus*, or the new kind of historicism, refers to contextualist approaches in contemporary philosophy. In order to prevent another misunderstanding, I would like to make it clear that I am not concerned with the recent trends in literary studies called new historicism.

3. I retain the format of a lecture without the usual armory of footnotes and the like.

4. This view is shared by Karl Jaspers, *Die grossen Philosophen* (München 1957).

5. Richard Rorty, "Relativism: Finding and Making," this volume, p. 36.

6. Ibid., p. 34.

7. Ibid., p. 40.

8. Ibid., p. 44.

9. Here Professor Rorty refers to comments made by Jürgen Habermas which have not been included in the present volume. These comments are included in the videotape of the original event. For information, contact The Foundation of The Institute of Philosophy and Sociology, ul. Nowy Swiat 72, 00–330 Warsaw, Poland, *Eds.*

Chapter 2

The Challenge of Relativism

RICHARD RORTY: RELATIVISM—FINDING AND MAKING

The term "relativist" is applied to philosophers who agree with Nietzsche that "'Truth' is the will to be master over the multiplicity of sensations." The term "relativist" is also applied to philosophers who agree with William James that "the 'true' is simply the expedient in the way of believing" and to those who agree with Thomas Kuhn that science should not be thought of as moving toward an accurate representation of the way the world is in itself. More generally, philosophers are called "relativists" when they do not accept the Greek distinction between the way things are in themselves and the relations which they have to other things, and in particular to human needs and interests.

Philosophers who, like myself, eschew this Greek distinction must abandon the traditional philosophical project of finding something stable which will serve as a criterion for judging the transitory products of our transitory needs and interests. This means, for example, that we cannot employ the Kantian distinction between morality and prudence. We have to give up the idea that there are unconditional, transcultural moral obligations, obligations rooted in an unchanging, ahistorical, human nature. This attempt to put aside both Plato and Kant is the bond which links the post-Nietzschean tradition in European philosophy with the pragmatic tradition in American philosophy.

The philosopher I most admire, and of whom I should most like to think of myself as a disciple, is John Dewey. Dewey was one of the founders of American pragmatism. He was a thinker who spent sixty years trying to get us out from under the thrall of Plato and Kant. Dewey was often denounced as a relativist, and so am I. But of course we pragmatists never call ourselves relativists. Usually, we define ourselves in negative terms. We call ourselves "anti-Platonists," "anti-metaphysicians," or "anti-foundationalists." Equally, however, our opponents almost never call themselves "Platonists" or "metaphysicians" or "foundationalists." They usually call themselves defenders of common sense or of reason.

Predictably, each side in this quarrel tries to define the terms of the quarrel in a way favorable to itself. Nobody wants to be called a Platonist, just as nobody wants to be called a relativist or an irrationalist. We so-called "relativists" refuse, predictably, to admit that we are enemies of reason and common sense. We say that we are only criticizing some antiquated, specifically philosophical dogmas. But, of course, what we call dogmas are exactly what our opponents call "common sense." Adherence to these dogmas is what they call "being rational." So discussion between us and our opponents tends to get bogged down in, for example, the question whether the slogan "truth is correspondence to the intrinsic nature of reality" expresses common sense, or is just a bit of outdated Platonist jargon.

The question is whether this slogan embodies an obvious truth which philosophy must respect and protect, or instead simply puts forward one philosophical view among others. Our opponents say that the correspondence theory of truth is so obvious, so self-evident, that it is merely perverse to question it. We say that this theory is barely intelligible and of no particular importance—that it is not so much a theory as a slogan which we have been mindlessly chanting for centuries. We pragmatists think that we might stop chanting it without any harmful consequences.

One way to describe this impasse is to say that we "relativists" claim that many of the things which common sense thinks are found or discovered are really made or invented. Scientific and moral truths, for example, are described by our opponents as "objective," meaning that they are in some sense out there waiting to be recognized by us human beings. So when our Platonist or Kantian opponents are tired of calling us "relativists" they call us "subjectivists" or "social constructionists." On their picture of the situation, we are claiming to have discovered that something which was supposed to come from outside us really comes from inside us. They think of us as saying that what was previously thought to be objective has turned out to be merely subjective.

But we anti-Platonists must not accept this way of formulating the issue. For if we do, we shall be in serious trouble. If we take the distinction between making and finding at face value, our opponents will be able to ask us an awkward question, namely, have we discovered the surprising fact that what was thought to be objective is actually subjective, or have we invented it? If we claim to have discovered it, if we say that it is an objective fact that truth is subjective, we are in danger of contradicting ourselves. If we say that we invented it, we seem to be being merely whimsical. Why should anybody take our invention seriously? If truths are merely convenient fictions, what about the truth of the claim that that is what they are? Is that too a convenient fiction? Convenient for what? For whom?

I think it is important that we who are accused of relativism stop using the distinctions between finding and making, discovery and invention, objective and subjective. We should not let ourselves be described as subjectivists or social constructionists. We cannot formulate our point in terms of a distinction between what is outside us and what is inside us. We must repudiate the vocabulary our opponents use and not let them impose it upon us.

To say that we must repudiate this vocabulary is to say, once again, that we must avoid Platonism and metaphysics, in that wide sense of metaphysics in which Heidegger said that metaphysics is Platonism. Whitehead was making the same point when he said that all of Western philosophy is a series of footnotes to Plato: We do not call an inquiry "philosophical" unless it revolves around some of the distinctions which Plato drew.

The distinction between the found and the made is a version of that between the absolute and the relative, between something which is what it is apart from its relations to other things and something whose nature depends upon those relations. In the course of the centuries, this distinction has become central to what Derrida calls "the metaphysics of presence"—the search for a "full presence beyond the reach of play," an absolute beyond the reach of relationality. So if we wish to abandon that metaphysics, we must stop distinguishing between the absolute and the relative. We anti-Platonists cannot permit ourselves to be called "relativists," since that description begs the central question. That central question is about the utility of the vocabulary which we inherited from Plato and Aristotle.

Our opponents like to suggest that to abandon that vocabulary is to abandon rationality—that to be rational consists precisely in respecting the distinctions between the absolute and the relative, the found and the made, object and subject, nature and convention, reality and appearance. We pragmatists reply that if that were what rationality is, then no doubt we are, indeed, irrationalists. But of course we go on to add that being an irrationalist in that sense is not to be incapable of argument. We irrationalists do not foam at the mouth and behave like animals. We simply refuse to talk in a certain way, the Platonic way. The views we hope to persuade people to accept cannot be stated in Platonic terminology. So our efforts at persuasion must take the form of gradual inculcation of new ways of speaking, rather than of straightforward argumentation within old ways of speaking.

To sum up what I have said so far, we pragmatists shrug off charges that we are "relativists" or "irrationalists" by saying that these charges presuppose precisely the distinctions we reject. If we have to have a snappy way of describing ourselves, perhaps it would be best for us to call ourselves antidualists. This does not, of course, mean that we are against every example of what Derrida calls "binary oppositions." We can perfectly well admit that we shall always have a use for such oppositions: Dividing the world up into the good "x's" and the bad "non-x's" will always be an indispensable tool of inquiry. But we are against a certain specific set of distinctions, the Platonic distinctions. We have to admit that these distinctions have become part of Western common sense, but we do not regard this as a sufficient argument for retaining them.

So far I have been speaking of "we so-called relativists" and of "we anti-Platonists." But now I need to become more specific and name names. As I said at the outset, the group of philosophers I have in mind includes a tradition of post-Nietzschean European philosophy and also a tradition of post-Darwinian American philosophy, the tradition of pragmatism. The great names of the first tradition include Heidegger, Sartre, Gadamer, Derrida, and Foucault. The great names of the second tradition include James, Dewey, Kuhn, Quine, Putnam, and Davidson. All of these philosophers have been fiercely attacked as relativists.

Both traditions have attempted to cast doubt on the Kantian and Hegelian distinction between subject and object, on the Cartesian distinctions which Kant and Hegel used to formulate their problematic, and on the Greek distinctions which provided the framework for Descartes's own thought. The most important thing that links the two traditions together is suspicion of the same set of Greek distinctions, the distinctions which make it possible, natural, and almost inevitable to ask, Found or made?, Absolute or relative?, Real or apparent?

Before saying more about what binds these two traditions together, however, I should say a little about what separates them. Although the European tradition owes much to Darwin by way of Nietzsche and Marx, European philosophers have typically distinguished quite sharply between what empirical scientists do and what philosophers do. Philosophers in this tradition often sneer at "naturalism" and "empiricism" and "reductionism." They sometimes condemn recent Anglophone philosophy without a hearing because they assume it to be infected by these diseases.

The American pragmatist tradition, by contrast, has made a point of breaking down the distinctions between philosophy, science, and politics. Its representatives often describe themselves as "naturalists," though they deny that they are reductionists or empiricists. Their objection to both traditional British empiricism and the scientistic reductionism characteristic of the Vienna Circle is precisely that neither is sufficiently naturalistic. In my perhaps chauvinistic view, we Americans have been more consistent than the Europeans, for American philosophers have realized that the idea of a distinctive, autonomous, cultural activity called "philosophy" becomes dubious when the Greek vocabulary which has dominated that activity is called into question. When Platonic dualisms go, the distinction between philosophy and the rest of culture is in danger.

Another way of exhibiting the difference between the two traditions is to say that the Europeans have typically put forward a distinctive, new, post-Nietzschean "method" for philosophers to employ. Thus in early Heidegger and early Sartre we find talk of "phenomenological ontology," in late Heidegger of something rather mysterious and wonderful called "Thinking," in Gadamer of "hermeneutics," and in Foucault of "the archaeology of knowledge" and of "genealogy." Only Derrida seems free from this temptation; his early use of the term "grammatology" was evanescent whimsy, rather than a serious attempt to proclaim the discovery of a new philosophical method or strategy.

By contrast, the Americans have not been much given to such methodological proclamations. Dewey, it is true, talked a lot about bringing "scientific method" into philosophy, but he never explained what this method was, nor what it was supposed to add to the virtues of curiosity, open-mindedness, and conversability. James sometimes spoke of "the pragmatic method," but this meant little more than the insistence on pressing the anti-Platonist question, "Do our purported theoretical differences make any difference to practice?" That insistence was not so much the employment of a method as the assumption of a skeptical attitude toward traditional philosophical problems and vocabularies. Quine, Putnam, and Davidson are all labelled "analytic philosophers," but none of the three thinks of himself as practicing a method called "conceptual analysis," nor any other method. The so-called "post-positivistic" version of analytic philosophy which these three philosophers have helped to create is notably free of the worship of method.

The various contemporary contributors to the pragmatist tradition are not much inclined to insist either on the distinctive nature of philosophy or on the preeminent place of philosophy within culture as a whole. None of them believe that philosophers think, or should think, in ways dramatically different from the ways in which physicists or politicians think. They would all agree with Thomas Kuhn that science, like politics, is problem solving. But the main problem which they want to solve is the origin of the problems which the philosophical tradition has bequeathed to us: Why, they ask, are the standard, textbook problems of philosophy both so intriguing and so barren? Why are philosophers, now as in Cicero's day, still arguing inconclusively, tramping round and round the same dialectical circles, never convincing each other but still able to attract students?

This question, the question of the nature of the problems which the Greeks, Descartes, Kant, and Hegel have bequeathed to us, leads us back to the distinction between finding and making. The philosophical tradition has insisted that these problems are found, in the sense that they are inevitably encountered by any reflective mind. The pragmatist tradition has often insisted that they are made—are artificial rather than natural—and can be unmade, dissolved, by using a different vocabulary than the one the philosophical tradition has used. But such distinctions between the found and the made, the natural and the artificial are, as I have already said, not distinctions we pragmatists should use. So it would be better for us pragmatists to say simply that the vocabulary in which the traditional problems of Western philosophy were formulated was useful at one time but is no longer so useful. Putting the matter in that way would obviate the appearance of saying that whereas the tradition dealt with something that was not really there, we pragmatists are dealing with what *is* really there.

Of course, we pragmatists cannot say *that*, for we have no use for the reality–appearance distinction, any more than for the distinction between the found and the made. We hope to replace the reality–appearance distinction with the distinction between the more useful and the less useful. So we say that the vocabulary of Greek metaphysics and Christian theology—the vocabulary used in what Heidegger called "the onto-theological tradition"—was a useful one for our ancestors' purposes, but we have different purposes, which will be better served by employing a different vocabulary. Our ancestors have climbed up a ladder which we are now in a position to throw away. We can throw it away not because we have reached a final resting place, but because we have different problems to solve than those which perplexed our ancestors.

So far I have been sketching the pragmatists' attitudes toward their opponents and the difficulties they encounter in avoiding terms whose use would beg the question that is at issue between them and their opponents. Now I should like to describe in somewhat more detail how human inquiry looks from a pragmatist point of view—how it looks once one stops describing it as an attempt to correspond to the intrinsic nature of reality and starts describing it as an attempt to serve transitory purposes and solve transitory problems.

Pragmatists hope to break with the picture which, in Wittgenstein's words, "holds us captive"—the Cartesian–Lockean notion of a mind seeking to get in touch with a reality outside it. So they start with a Darwinian account of human beings as animals doing their best to cope with the environment—doing their best to develop tools which will enable them to enjoy more pleasure and less pain. Words are among the tools which these clever animals have developed.

There is no way in which tools can take one out of touch with reality. No matter whether the tool is a hammer or a gun or a belief or a statement, tool-using is part of the interaction of the organism with its environment. To see the employment of words as the use of tools to deal with the environment, rather than as an attempt to represent the intrinsic nature of that environment, is to repudiate the question of whether human minds are in touch with reality—the question asked by the epistemological skeptic. No organism, human or nonhuman, is ever more or less in touch with reality than any other organism. The very idea of "being out of touch with reality" presupposes the un-Darwinian, Cartesian picture of a mind which somehow swings free of the causal forces exerted on the body. The Cartesian mind is an entity whose relations with the rest of the universe are representational rather than causal. So to rid our thinking of the vestiges of Cartesianism, to become fully Darwinian in our thinking, we need to stop thinking of words as representations and to start thinking of them as nodes in the causal network which binds the organism together with its environment.

Seeing language and inquiry in this biologistic way permits us to discard the picture of the human mind as an interior space within which the human person is located. As the American philosopher of mind Daniel Dennett has argued, it is only this picture of a "Cartesian Theater" (as he calls it) which makes us think that there is a big philosophical or scientific problem about the nature or the origin of consciousness. We can substitute another picture for the one Descartes gave us: This will be a picture of an adult human organism as one whose behavior is so complex that it can be predicted only by attributing intentional states—beliefs and desires—to the organism. On this account, beliefs and desires are not prelinguistic modes of consciousness, which may or may not be expressible in language. Nor are they names of immaterial events. Rather, they are what in philosophical jargon are called "sentential attitudes"—that is to say, dispositions on the part of organisms, or of computers, to assert or deny certain sentences. To attribute beliefs and desires to nonusers of language (such as dogs, infants, and thermostats) is, for us pragmatists, to speak metaphorically.

Pragmatists complement this biologistic approach with Charles Sanders Peirce's definition of a belief as a habit of action. On this definition, to ascribe a belief to someone is simply to say that he or she will tend to behave as I behave when I am willing to affirm the truth of a certain sentence. We ascribe beliefs to things which use, or can be imagined to use, sentences, but not to rocks and plants. This is not because the former have a special organ or capacity—consciousness—which the latter lack, but simply because the habits of action of rocks and plants are sufficiently familiar and simple that their behavior can be predicted without ascribing sentential attitudes to them.

On this view, when we utter such sentences as "I am hungry" we are not making external what was previously internal, but simply helping those around us to predict our future actions. Such sentences are not used to report events going on within the sealed inner room which is a person's consciousness. They are simply tools for coordinating our behavior with those of others. This is not to say that one can "reduce" mental states such as beliefs and desires to physiological or behavioral states. It is merely to say that there is no point in asking whether a belief represents reality, either mental reality or physical reality, accurately. That is, for pragmatists, not only a bad question, but the cause of much wasted philosophical energy.

The right question to ask is, For what purposes might it be useful to hold that belief? This is like the question, For what purposes would it be useful to load this program into my computer? On the view I am suggesting, a person's body is analogous to the computer's hardware, and his or her beliefs and desires are analogous to the software. Nobody knows or cares whether a given piece of computer software represents reality accurately. All we care about is whether it is the software which, among programs currently available, will most efficiently accomplish a certain task. Analogously, pragmatists think that the question to ask about our beliefs is not whether they are about reality or merely about appearance, but simply whether they are the best available habits of action for gratifying our desires.

On this view, to say that a belief is, as far as we know, true is to say that no alternative belief is, as far as we know, a better habit of acting. When we say that our ancestors believed, falsely, that the sun went around the earth and that we believe, truly, that the earth goes round the sun, we are saying that we have a better tool than our ancestors did. Our ancestors might rejoin that their tool enabled them to believe in the literal truth of the Christian Scriptures, whereas ours does not. Our reply has to be, I think, that the benefits of modern astronomy and of space travel outweigh the advantages of Christian fundamentalism. The argument between us and our medieval ancestors should not be about which of us has gotten the universe right. It should be about the point of holding views about the motion of heavenly bodies, the ends to be achieved by the use of certain tools. Confirming the truth of Scripture is one such aim, space travel is another.

Another way to make this last point is to say that we pragmatists cannot make sense of the idea that we should pursue truth for its own sake. We cannot regard truth as a goal of inquiry. The purpose of inquiry is to achieve agreement among human beings about what to do, to bring about consensus on the ends to be achieved and the means to be used to achieve those ends. Inquiry that does not achieve coordination of behavior is not inquiry, but simply wordplay. To argue for a certain theory about the microstructure of material bodies or about the proper balance of powers between branches of government is to argue about what we should do: how we should use the tools at our disposal in order to make technological or political progress. So for pragmatists, there is no sharp break between natural science and social science, nor between social science and politics, nor between politics, philosophy, and literature. All areas of culture are parts of the same endeavor to make life better. There is no deep split between theory and practice, because on a pragmatist view all so-called "theory" which is not wordplay is always already practice.

To treat beliefs not as representations but as habits of action, and words not as representations but as tools, is to make it pointless to ask, Am I discovering or inventing, making or finding? There is no point in dividing the organism's interaction with the environment up in this way. Consider an example. We normally say that a bank account is a social construction rather than an object in the natural world, whereas a giraffe is an object in the natural world rather than a social construction. Bank accounts are made, giraffes are found. Now the truth in this view is simply that if there had been no human beings there would still have been giraffes, whereas there would have been no bank accounts. But this causal independence of giraffes from humans does not mean that giraffes are what they are apart from human needs and interests.

On the contrary, we describe giraffes in the way we do, as giraffes, because of our needs and interests. We speak a language which includes the word "giraffe" because it suits our purposes to do so. The same goes for words like "organ," "cell," "atom," and so on—the names of the parts out of which giraffes are made, so to speak. *All* the descriptions we give of things are descriptions suited to *our* purposes. No sense can be made, we pragmatists argue, of the claim that some of these descriptions pick out "natural kinds"—that they cut nature at the joints. The line between a giraffe and the surrounding air is clear enough if you are a human being interested in hunting for meat. If you are a language-using ant or amoeba or a space voyager observing us from far above that line is not so clear, and it is not clear that you will need or have a word for "giraffe" in your language. More generally, it is not clear that any of the millions of ways of describing the piece of space-time occupied by what we call a giraffe is any closer to the way things are in themselves than any of the others. Just as it seems pointless to ask whether a giraffe is really a collection of atoms or really a collection of actual and possible sensations in human sense organs, or really something else, so the question "Are we describing it as it really is?" is one we never need to ask. All we need to know is whether some competing description might be more useful for some of our purposes.

The relativity of descriptions to purposes is the pragmatists' principal argument for their antirepresentational view of knowledge—the view that inquiry aims at utility for us rather than an accurate account of how things are in themselves. Because every belief we have must be formulated in some language or other and because languages are not attempts to copy what is out there, but rather are tools for dealing with what is out there, there is no way to divide 'the contribution to our knowledge made by the object' from 'the contribution made by our subjectivity'. Both the words we use and our willingness to affirm certain sentences using those words and not others are the product of fantastically complex causal connections between human organisms and the rest of the universe. There is no way to divide up this web of causal connections so as to compare the relative amounts of subjectivity and objectivity in a given belief. There is no way, as Wittgenstein said, to come between language and its object, to divide the giraffe in itself from our ways of talking about giraffes. As Hilary Putnam, the leading contemporary pragmatist, has put it: "Elements of what we call 'language' or 'mind' penetrate so deeply into reality that the very project of representing ourselves as being 'mappers' of something 'language-independent' is fatally compromised from the start."[1]

The Platonist dream of perfect knowledge is the dream of stripping ourselves clean of everything that comes from inside us and opening ourselves without reservation to what is outside us. But this distinction between inside and outside, as I have said earlier, is one we cannot make once we adopt a Darwinian biologistic self-image. If the Platonist is going to insist on that distinction, he or she has to have an epistemology which does not link up in any interesting way with any other discipline or area of culture. He or she will end up with an account of knowledge which turns its back on the rest of science. This amounts to making human knowledge into a kind of miracle—the kind of miracle which only metaphysics, as opposed to natural science, could explain.

The suggestion that everything we say and do and believe is a matter of fulfilling human needs and interests might seem simply a way of formulating the secularism of the Enlightenment—a way of saying that human beings are on their own and have no supernatural light to guide them to the truth. But of course the Enlightenment replaced the idea of such supernatural guidance with the idea of a quasi-divine faculty called "reason." It is this idea which American pragmatists and post-Nietzschean European philosophers are attacking. What seems most shocking about their criticisms of this idea is not their description of natural science as an attempt to manage reality rather than to represent it. Rather, it is their description of moral choice as always a matter of compromise between competing goods rather than as a choice between the absolutely right and the absolutely wrong.

Controversies between foundationalists and antifoundationalists in the theory of knowledge look like the sort of merely scholastic quarrels which can safely be left to philosophy professors. But quarrels about the character of moral choice seem more important. We stake our sense of who we are on the outcome of such choices. So we do not like to be told that our choices were between alternative goods rather than between good and evil. When philosophy professors start saying that there is nothing absolutely wrong or absolutely right, the topic of relativism begins to get interesting. The debates between the pragmatists and their opponents, or the post-Nietzscheans and theirs, begin to look too important to be left to philosophy professors. Everybody wants to get in on the act.

This is why philosophers like myself find ourselves denounced in magazines and newspapers which one might have thought oblivious to our existence. These denunciations claim that unless the youth is raised to believe in moral absolutes and in objective truth, civilization is doomed. Unless the younger generation has the same attachment to firm moral principles as we have, these magazine and newspaper articles say, the struggle for human freedom and human decency will be over. When we philosophy teachers read this sort of article, we find ourselves being told that we have enormous power over the future of humankind. For all it will take to overturn centuries of moral progress, these articles suggest, is a generation which accepts the doctrines of moral relativism, accepts the views common to Nietzsche and Dewey.

Dewey and Nietzsche of course disagreed about a lot of things. Nietzsche thought that the happy, prosperous masses who would inhabit Dewey's social-democratic utopia were "the last men"; worthless creatures incapable of greatness. Nietzsche was as instinctively antidemocratic in his politics as Dewey was instinctively democratic. But the two men agree not only on the nature of knowledge but on the nature of moral choice. Dewey said that every evil is a rejected good. William James said that every human need has a prima facie right to be gratified, and the only reason for refusing to gratify it is that it conflicts with another human need. Nietzsche would have entirely agreed. He would have phrased this point in terms of competition between bearers of the will to power, whereas James and Dewey would have found the term "power," with its sadistic overtones, a bit misleading. But these three philosophers made identical criticisms of Enlightenment—and specifically Kantian—attempts to view moral principles as the product of a special faculty called "reason." They all thought that such attempts were disingenuous attempts to keep something like God alive in the midst of a secular culture.

Critics of moral relativism think that unless there is something absolute, something which shares God's implacable refusal to yield to human weakness, we have no reason to go on resisting evil. For if evil is merely a lesser good, if all moral choice is a compromise between conflicting goods, then, they say, there is no point in moral struggle. The lives of those who have died resisting injustice seem to become pointless. But to us pragmatists moral struggle is continuous with the Darwinian struggle for existence, and no sharp break divides the unjust from the imprudent, the evil from the inexpedient. What matters for pragmatists is devising ways of diminishing human suffering and increasing human equality, increasing the ability of all human children to start life with an equal chance of happiness. This goal is not written in the stars and is no more an expression of what Kant called "pure practical reason" than it is the Will of God. It is a goal worth dying for, but it does not require backup from supernatural forces.

The pragmatist view of what opponents of pragmatism call "firm moral principles" is that such principles are abbreviations of past practices—ways of summing up the habits of the ancestors whom we most admire. For example, Mill's greater-happiness principle and Kant's categorical imperative are ways of reminding ourselves of certain social customs: those of certain parts of the Christian West, parts of the culture which has been, at least in words if not in deeds, more egalitarian than any other. The Christian doctrine that all members of the species are brothers and sisters is the religious way of saying what Mill and Kant said in secular terms: that considerations of family membership, sex, race, religious creed, and the like should not prevent us from trying to do unto others as we would have them do to us—should not prevent us from thinking of them as people like ourselves, deserving the respect which we ourselves hope to enjoy.

But there are other firm moral principles than those which epitomize egalitarianism. One such principle is that dishonor brought to a woman of one's family must be paid for with blood. Another is that it would be better to have no son than to have one who is homosexual. Those of us who would like to put a stop to the blood-feuds and the gay-bashing to which such firm moral principles give rise call these principles "prejudices" rather than "insights." It would be nice if philosophers could give us assurance that the principles which we approve of, like Mill's and Kant's, are "rational" in a way that the principles of the blood-revengers and the gay-bashers are not. But to say that they are more rational seems to me just another way of saying that they are more universalistic, that they treat the differences between women of one's own family and other women and the difference between gays and straights as relatively insignificant. But it is not clear that failure to mention particular groups of people is a mark of rationality.

To see this last point, consider the principle "Thou shalt not kill." This is admirably universal, but is it more or less rational than the principle "Do not kill unless you are a soldier defending your country, or are preventing a murder, or are a state executioner or a merciful practitioner of euthanasia"? I have no idea whether it is more or less rational, and for that reason I do not find the term "rational" useful in this area. If I am told that a controversial action which I have taken should be defended by being subsumed under a universal, rational principle, I may be able to dream up such a principle to fit the occasion. But sometimes I may only be able to say, Well, it seemed like the best thing to do at the time, all things considered. It is not clear that the latter defense is less rational than some universal-sounding principle which I have dreamed up ad hoc to justify my action. It is not clear that the moral dilemmas which we confront in a rapidly changing world—dilemmas having to do with population control, the rationing of health care, and the like—should wait upon the formulation of principles for their solution.

As we pragmatists see it, the idea that there must be such a legitimating principle lurking behind every right action amounts to the idea that there is something like a universal, supernational court of law before which we stand. We know that the best societies are those which are governed by laws rather than by tyrants or mobs. Without the rule of law, we say, human life is turned over to emotion and to violence. This makes us think that there must be a sort of invisible tribunal of reason, administering laws which we all, somewhere deep down inside, recognize as binding upon us. Something like this was Kant's understanding of moral obligation. But, once again, the Kantian picture of what human beings are like cannot easily be reconciled with history or with biology. Both teach us that the development of societies ruled by laws rather than men was a slow, late, fragile, contingent, evolutionary achievement.

Dewey thought that Hegel was right, as opposed to Kant, when Hegel insisted that universal moral principles were useful only insofar as they abbreviated the historical development of a particular society—a society whose institutions would give content to an otherwise empty formula. Recently, Michael Walzer, a political philosopher best known for his earlier work *Spheres of Justice*, has come to Hegel's and Dewey's defense. In his new book *Thick and Thin*, Waltzer argues that we should not think of the customs and institutions of particular societies as accidental accretions around a common core of universal moral rationality—the transcultural moral law. Rather we should think of the thick set of customs and institutions as prior and as what commands primary moral allegiance. The thin morality which can be abstracted out of the various thick moralities is not made up of the commandments of a universally shared human faculty called "reason." Such thin resemblances between these thick moralities as may exist—or may be developed—are contingent; as contingent as the resemblances between the adaptive organs of diverse biological species.

Those who adopt the anti-Kantian stance common to Hegel, Dewey, and Walzer and are asked to defend the thick morality of the society with which they identify themselves will not be able to do so by talking about the rationality of their moral views. Rather, they will have to talk about the various concrete advantages of their society's practices over those of other societies. Discussion of the relative advantages of different thick moralities will, obviously, be as inconclusive as discussion of the relative superiority of a beloved book or person over another person's beloved book or person. The idea of a universally shared source of truth called "reason" or "human nature" is, for us pragmatists, just the idea that such discussion ought to be capable of being made conclusive. We see this idea as a misleading way of expressing a hope, which we share, that the human race as a whole should gradually come together in a global community, a community which incorporates most of the thick morality of the European industrialized democracies. It is misleading because it suggests that the aspiration to that community is somehow built into every member of the biological species. This seems to us pragmatists to be like the suggestion that the aspiration to be an anaconda is somehow built into all reptiles, or that the aspiration to be an anthropoid is somehow built into all mammals. This is why we pragmatists see the charge of relativism as simply the charge that we see luck where our critics insist on seeing destiny. We think that the utopian world community envisaged by the Charter of the United Nations and the Helsinki Declaration of Human Rights is no more the destiny of humanity than is an atomic holocaust or the replacement of democratic governments by feuding warlords. If either of the latter is what the future holds, our species will have been unlucky, but it will not have been irrational. It will not have failed to live up to its moral obligations. It will simply have missed a chance to be happy.

I do not know how to argue the question of whether it is better to see human beings in this biologistic way or to see them in a way more like Plato's or Kant's. So I do not know how to give anything like a conclusive argument for the view which my critics call "relativism" and which I prefer to call "antidualism." It is certainly not enough for my side to appeal to Darwin and ask our opponents how they can avoid an appeal to the supernatural. That way of stating the issue begs many questions. It is certainly not enough for my opponents to say that a biologistic view strips human beings of their dignity and their self-respect. That too begs most of the questions at issue. I suspect that all that either side can do is to restate its case over and over again, in context after context. The controversy between those who see both our species and our democratic society as a lucky accident and those who find an immanent teleology in both is too radical to permit of being judged from some neutral standpoint.

RICHARD RORTY: ON MORAL OBLIGATION, TRUTH, AND COMMON SENSE

I shall discuss Jürgen Habermas's objections in reverse order, starting with his last and working backward.[2]

I see the distinction between morality and self-interest as the distinction between my sense of myself as part of a group united by reciprocal loyalty and my sense of myself as an isolated individual. So I see the answer to the question, How could we convince people to accept these excessive demands? as By enlarging their sense of who counts as one of "us" as a member of our community of loyalty.

We all start out thinking of ourselves as a member of some group, at least of a family. This membership gives rise to conflicts, which cause us to say something like, It would be nice for me, but it would be disastrous for the family, so, of course, I cannot do it. We then, if we are fortunate, come to be able to reach out beyond the family to the village, the tribe, the nation, and so on. I see moral progress as people's imaginative ability to identify with people whom their ancestors had not been able to identify with—people of different religions, people on the other side of the world, people who initially seem disturbingly different from "us."

The Kantian tradition says that we are unconditionally obligated to feel a sense of moral community with all other rational agents. I find that an unhelpful saying. I am not sure I can tell a rational agent when I see one, but I can distinguish the beings which seem enough like me to let me to imagine using persuasion rather than force in my dealings with them. The grasp of this likeness helps me think of them as members of a possible moral community.

I think that Hume, rather than Kant, shows us how we get people to form larger groups: namely, by appealing to sentimentality, and thereby inviting imaginative identification. Consider the example of emotional attraction between people of different sexes and different cultures. If you want to break down xenophobia, one practical way to do so is to encourage such emotional attraction by making intermarriage legitimate and easy. If you cannot, initially, get your people to marry these strangers, you can at least tell stories about them, stories in which imagination takes the place of actual physical relationships.

This was the role of reformist social novels such as *Uncle Tom's Cabin*. White Americans were, in the middle of the last century, not willing to marry black Americans. But they were, mercifully, at least willing to read novels about them. After reading Stowe's novel, the suggestion "perhaps the blacks are much like ourselves" became slightly more acceptable. If you told most white Americans before the American Civil War that the blacks were rational agents in Kant's sense, they would not get your point. They would insist that these creatures are *black* and that that is a good enough reason to treat them very differently. Novels then and intermarriage now make it harder to see skin color as a reason for exclusion from the moral community.

So I think Habermas sets things up the wrong way when he puts things in terms of self-interest versus obligation. He is following the example of Plato, who set things up the wrong way in the *Republic* by saying that we had to choose between Thrasymachean selfishness and recollection of the Form of the Good. I think Hume got things right when he said that the interesting contrast is between people with whom you can feel at home and people with whom you cannot feel at home—or between people you can imagine being and people you simply *cannot* imagine being.

This is why I think of imagination and sentiment, rather than reason (considered as the ability to argue), as the faculties which do the most to make moral progress possible. I do not want to be a neo-Aristotelian, I want to be a neo-Humean. There is a big difference. The neo-Humean view is best set forth in a recent book by the American philosopher Annette Baier, *Moral Prejudices*. Baier urges that we substitute justified trust for obligation as our fundamental moral category. She takes the trust–obligation distinction to epitomize the Hume–Kant distinction. Hume takes trust, the kind of relation that holds between members of a nuclear family, to be the fundamental moral phenomenon. Kant takes law as the fundamental moral phenomenon. That seems to me much more important than the difference between Aristotle and Kant.

That is all I will say about moral obligation. Now, let me come to truth. I think Habermas is right that the difference between the attempt common to him, Putnam, and Peirce—the attempt to idealize the notion of rational acceptability—and my attempt to build utopian social hope is not all that great.

My attempt amounts to thinking of the contrast between the merely justified and the true not as the contrast between the actual and the ideal, but simply as the contrast between justification to us as we are here and now and justification to a superior version of ourselves, the version we hope our descendants will exemplify.

Consider what I call the "cautionary use of truth," the use of 'true' in the phrase "unjustifiable to all of you but maybe true anyway" (or as in the case of Luther, "unjustifiable to you but *certainly* true anyway [italics added]"). I think of the contrast which is drawn in such phrases as a contrast between this age of the world and a possible future, better, age of the world—not "the end of inquiry" or "the ideal cognitive situation," but just a better age than ours.

I take Luther to have been saying something like this: "I speak to you here at Worms not as someone who has much hope of persuading you, not as somebody propounding arguments starting from shared premises. Rather, I stand before you as the prophet of an age struggling to be born, of a world yet to be disclosed." More generally, I think that we can always say, when urging a disputed claim, that at present there is too little justification for believing this, but a world may arise in which it seems just common sense. Alternatively, we can always say, that at present there is every justification for believing the view I am denying, but a world may be disclosed in which this proposition is not even a candidate for justification, in which the whole question of this proposition's truth is no longer raised. So I think of the cautionary use of 'true', the use in which it swings free of present practices of justification, as the voice of prophecy. This voice says, Some day the world will be changed, and then this proposition may turn out to be true. That romantic hope for another world which is yet to come is at the heart of the anti-Platonist's quest for spiritual perfection.

I am tempted to follow Derrida in thinking of such hope as marking a fundamental difference between the Jews and the Greeks. I take Platonism and Greek thought generally to say, The set of candidates for truth is already here, and all the reasons which might be given for and against their truth are also already here; all that remains is to argue the matter out. I think of romantic (or, for Derrida, Judaic) hope as saying, Some day all of these truth candidates, and all of these notions of what counts as a good reason for believing them, may be obsolete; for a much better world is to come—one in which we shall have wonderful new truth candidates. If one holds the Greek view, then it is reasonable to define truth in terms of idealized rational acceptability in the manner of Habermas, Peirce, and Putnam. But that definition will be useless once one starts thinking of languages and truth-candidates as constantly in the process of change.

Obviously, there is a tension between this romantic hope and actual day-to-day striving for democratic consensus. Professor Habermas looks principally at the need for consensus in this world now, whereas I am obsessed by the possibility of the disclosure of new worlds. My deep wish for everything to be wonderfully, utterly changed keeps me from saying that truth is idealized rational acceptability. After all, you can only idealize what you have already got. But maybe there is something you cannot even dream of yet.

I think that if Luther had said "An idealized Diet of Worms would agree with me," we should not have been able to make much sense of his remark. For what would an idealized Diet of Worms look like? Instead, I think of him as saying, "Some day you people here at Worms are not even going to be relevant."

That prediction was pretty much right, as it turns out. Such disclosures of new worlds have in fact happened in the course of recorded history. When the Greeks first envisaged democratic government, when early modern atomists took Democritus seriously and wondered if the world might not indeed be just atoms and void, when proto-Darwinians suggested that the difference between us and the brutes was merely in complexity of behavior, and when Freud suggested the connection between conscience and sex, they were saying things that were pretty close to absurd, that were hardly even candidates for truth. But these almost absurd claims became the common sense of later times.

These new worlds take a long time to achieve their full glory. Though Darwin has been dead for a hundred years, it will probably take us at least as long to feel comfortable with Darwin as it took us to feel comfortable with seventeenth-century physics. The human self-image that Darwin makes possible is very different from the various possible pre-Darwinian images. When Hobbes wrote *Leviathan*, the change he envisaged in our sense of who we are was a very crude attempt to come to terms with Galilean corpuscularianism; but by 1810, after Kant and Fichte, we had much more sophisticated ways of coming to terms with the new science. Spencer stands to Darwin as Hobbes stood to Galileo. Spencer was a first, very crude attempt to come to terms with Darwin. Dewey was far more sophisticated than Spencer, just as Leibnitz and Kant were far more sophisticated than Hobbes, even though they were dealing with the same problem. I think we have not even begun to assimilate Freud. Freud has been dead for fifty years but we intellectuals are barely beginning to come to terms with Freud.

It is time for me to stop talking. Perhaps I can sum up by trying to answer Professor Habermas's question, "Why change common sense?" I can give three answers. First, we have it on our intellectual conscience to come to terms with Darwin and Freud, and we have not really done that yet. Second, we are still obsessed with Greek dualisms, dualisms which have become mere philosophical nuisances. Third, maybe Darwin was a glimpse of a new moral world waiting to be disclosed. We will never find out unless we try. I think that the romantic hope of substituting new common sense for old common sense is a reason for skepticism about the latter. Such hope amounts to saying the world is still young. The cultural evolution of our species is just beginning. We do not have any idea yet of the possibilities, but we need to take full advantage of people like Luther, Copernicus, Galileo, Darwin, and Freud, because they give us our chances. They are our chances to transform the candidates for truth and thereby make previous patterns of justification obsolete.

LESZEK KOLAKOWSKI: A REMARK ON RORTY

Let us not talk about the "intrinsic nature of reality" and the need to get rid of this concept. In everyday parlance, when we say "It rains," we do not keep in mind an intrinsic nature of reality in which it rains. We have in mind no more than that "it is the case that it rains." Does such a saying imply a hidden Platonism, a belief in a transcendental, transcultural truth? if it is the case that it rains, is it true for every rational creature? No, and perhaps Rorty would not aver it does. He might accept the common manner of speaking (it is the case that it rains) but reject a particular meaning which some philosophers, in his view, attribute to it, namely an idea of reality, independent from human thought and language, a reality in which it is true and it is eternally true that it rains right now. Rorty's point, if I understand him properly, is negative: He wants to do away with any epistemology, with Cartesian, Lockean, and Kantian questions, rather than suggest or invent an epistemology of his own. He prefers not to assume the title of a "relativist" who says that what we call true is "subjective" or "invented," because this would entangle him in impossible problems; he simply would like to destroy some philosophical habits (adaequatio, correspondence, etc.). Since his proposals seem to change nothing about the way people communicate with each other in everyday life or in science, they can be of concern only to a handful of philosophers (this is not an objection) who keep sticking to the sterile tradition which legitimizes the subject-object opposition as well as the idea of a reality simply being there and waiting for discoverers. The distinction we need and in fact employ, according to Rorty, is that of more useful versus less useful (or useless, presumably, or harmful).

That the question is of interest only to a few philosophers and has no bearing upon life and the thinking of other people does not make it empty. To be sure, philosophers talk about things they have always been talking about—God, truth, justice, good and evil, and so on—whereas professors of philosophy, as Gilson observed, talk about philosophy. Both Rorty and myself belong rather to the class of professors. We cannot help it.

Rorty's suggestions are not new, certainly, and he knows that. That the Cartesian subject-object distinction is not needed and not justifiable in terms of either common sense or scientific discourse was a contention repeatedly made in the nineteenth century by German and Austrian philosophers, such as Mach and Avenarius, among others (one should mention that whereas the former's writings display a praiseworthy clarity and precision, the latter built an extremely intricate language of his own, making his work almost impenetrable; sometimes I think that I am the last living person on earth who ever read Avenarius). They both criticized the idea of a material object mysteriously sneaking into the mind of a subject-observer and leaving there its disincarnated likeness. They saw no use in sticking to the traditional concept of truth and argued that pragmatic criteria are good enough to settle all the problems of the credibility of knowledge and that we need nothing more. I am not really sure what American pragmatists added to this criticism.

I admit—and I have had the opportunity to say it on various occasions—that there is no absolute beginning in the cognitive process, no state of "epistemological innocence" and that our language is a collection of tools, rather than a reflection of the world; on those points I am largely in agreement with Rorty, all the time stressing that the critique of the cogito is three and a half centuries old.

Still, my agreement is not complete. When we employ pragmatic criteria of acceptability (and not 'truth'), we inevitably raise the question, Why?; why are pragmatic criteria good? And what are they properly? As I said in my remark on relativism, I have strong doubts about the criteria of "usefulness" (Rorty speaks even of "happiness," which I find horrifying) because of their vagueness and our inability to decide what, for whom, and on what time scale anything is useful or not. Criteria of efficacity and predictive power, though vague, are more precise, and we roughly know how to apply them. But even on the assumption that utilitarian criteria are clear enough and the rules of their applicability are known, a critic will pester the pragmatist with a further going question: Why does the pragmatist think that these criteria are good or better than any other? If this is his arbitrary decision, what reason do I have to support it? And if the criterion of usefulness is good (as Rorty suggests) because it is itself useful, the pragmatists' reasoning is circular and I see no intellectual argument to follow them.

The possible answer, "we do in fact apply utilitarian criteria, whether we know it or not," would not do; first because then all philosophical doctrines, epistemological principles of old, religious beliefs, and traditional theories which the pragmatists want to kill might turn out to be good—since they exist—according to the pragmatists' own criteria; second, because it would be difficult to prove the usefulness of many scientific theories or mathematical truths which enjoy the acceptance of scientists (William James's saying that we need a surplus of potentially useful truths—as he defines them—is of little help since it is not clear at all how we can assess the potential usefulness of a truth of which the actual usefulness is unknown and unprovable); third, because one cannot reasonably argue that the intended meaning of all our utterances is, as a matter of fact, practical and that, for instance, when I say "It rains," the intended meaning of this sentence is "I better take an umbrella when I go out." Indeed, I would find this sort of reduction absurd and unjustifiable.

Another possible way of avoiding circularity or infinite regression might consist in saying, in Wittgensteinian manner, that yes, all sentences in which we state the criteria of truth (or admissibility) are indeed meaningless but they have a therapeutic value ("the ladder" we can throw away, having climbed on it) and once we understand that (which we cannot, strictly speaking, as they are meaningless) we get rid of impossible epistemological and metaphysical questions. But it is impracticable and inefficient (and thus presumably meaningless in pragmatic terms) to tell humankind, Let's make a secret agreement to the effect that we will never ask epistemological questions and never explain why we do not ask them. Therefore, we have to pay a price for our therapy; we avoid circularity but we have to give a special meaning to our "ladder"; we transubstantiate it into a linguistic game; meanwhile, nobody asks whether the game is "true" or "false," since the question is absurd. Yes, we are rid of the infernal circularity but we are compelled to admit that in terms of "truth" any game is as good as any other and that pragmatists' criteria of acceptability are no better in any recognizable sense than the criteria which the metaphysicians of old tried to devise. And so pragmatism risks legitimizing all those metaphysical, religious, and epistemological occupations which to do away with was its main purpose, its raison d'être. We simply may not say, Dewey was right and Husserl was wrong; they just played different language games.

Moreover, pragmatism can provide a legitimacy to those occupations on logically prior grounds, that is to say, by applying its criteria of usefulness. Nobody can deny—James did not, of course—that religious beliefs are useful; therefore, they are legitimate. A pragmatist can say to believers, Your beliefs are legitimate because they are useful to you. But he cannot preach to them on any other ground, and it is impossible for believers to believe in God and to believe at the same time that they believe in God because this belief is useful. No, they believe in God because it is true that God exists.

This unpleasant and apparently insoluble conflict between two levels of language in pragmatist philosophy extends to all our beliefs, but in some of them it is of little cultural significance, whereas it is destructive in the realm of religion and morality. Assuming that I was convinced that the validity of sentences like "The atomic number of iron is 26" or "The Nile is the longest river" is defined by the benefits (or happiness perhaps? But what is there to be happy about?) which the belief in those sentences brings to me or to the human race, I have no reason to be disturbed or to worry about this explanation; indeed, nothing really changes in my intellectual equipment, in my emotions, or in practical affairs. The situation is different in the case of sentences like "The course of events is guided uninterruptedly by the divine providence"; or "To torture people is evil, to help people in their misery is good." Once I am convinced that the validity of those sentences is only utilitarian, and thus they carry no truth in the common meaning of this word, everything changes in my way of perceiving the world. My behavior is not altered when I learn that the meaning of the sentence "The Nile is the longest river" is in fact prescriptive (whatever that means). To be sure, one may argue that there is nothing wrong with the meaning of the sentence "Torture is evil" being prescriptive, since if it orders me to do anything, it is that I must not torture people; but I am perplexed and mentally insecure when I hear that there is no such real quality as "being evil," and that the prescription is useful or that it brings more happiness to mankind is by no means certain, even in the case just quoted. Shall we admit that the status of the prescription "Do not torture people" is the same as that of the norm "Keep the fork in the left hand and the knife in the right one," so that torturers dwell in another language game than those who forbid torture, not unlike people who observe European or Chinese table customs, respectively?

What I seek to say is not that I have compelling arguments to prove that "in the nature of things" there is indeed such a quality as "being evil" (even though I believe that there is). My point is only that apart from the perplexing problems arising from two levels of language, the pragmatist interpretation might have undesirable cultural consequences.

The third area which is probably difficult to a pragmatist to handle is mathematics. I admit that I believe that there are synthetic *a priori* judgments and that mathematical objects do exist. In believing this I am in good company (in which probably there are fewer philosophers than mathematicians; many of the latter know that they discover, rather than construct, their world), but this is not an irrefutable argument. I am not really knowledgeable enough to discuss this question. I guess that pragmatists can be happy with the belief that all mathematical propositions are tautologies (geometry is a separate case; Mach argued that some of its propositions are empirical and some tautological, whereas to Poincaré this was a matter of convention; there is no point in asking whether Euclidean geometry or the non-Euclidean ones are "true"). If they are not, pragmatists are in trouble. And the question is perplexing; nearly everything else in human affairs changes—physics, feminine fashions, literary styles, medicine, religious beliefs, architecture—but Euclid's proofs seem eternally valid. Why?

To the pragmatists, everything is a cultural product. By saying this they risk producing the same self-reference paradox: Pragmatism is as such as much a passing fashion as Platonism once was; and its claims to validity are not stronger. But is the simple proposition—beautifully proved by Euclid—that the series of prime numbers is infinite a matter of fashion as well? Or is it a tautology? And if so, what is the status of tautologies in the pragmatist interpretation? How could they be everlasting?

It is somewhat too easy to say poets once did not know rhymes, then they used rhymes for several centuries, then they again stopped using them, and it is pointless to ask whether rhymes are true or not and to extend this observation onto all products of human thought. Various realms of culture grew from different roots; one of them is the quest for truth. And if the root of philosophy is indeed a Platonic astonishment—astonishment at being—then the ultimate death of philosophy is unlikely. A trend which spreads and grows for a long time seems unstoppable to its contemporaries; they have the impression that its worldwide total victory is inevitable. But if there is a lesson in history, it says that such impressions are reckless and almost invariably false.

RICHARD RORTY: RESPONSE TO KOLAKOWSKI

Leszek Kolakowski and I differ about the implications of a view that we both accept: that "our language is a collection of tools, rather than a reflection of the world," and that we should therefore drop the notion that true statements correspond to the intrinsic nature of reality.

I take this view to imply that we should stop seeing the search for truth as distinct from the search for happiness, and that we can no longer contrast, as Kolakowski does, the utility of a belief with its "truth in the common meaning of the word." As I see it, once the opposition between correspondence and utility goes, so does the contrast between truth and utility.

Kolakowski, however, is horrified by my use of the term "happiness" and by my attempt to treat inquiry into what to believe as one more form of our unceasing attempt to increase pleasure and avoid pain. He sees the thesis about language-as-tools as a minor philosophical adjustment, the sort of change that has no cultural importance outside of the little circle of philosophy professors to which he and I belong. Despite his renunciation of truth-as-correspondence, he persists in contrasting "mere utility" with "truth."

I think we should view the substitution of metaphors of tool-using for those of mirroring and the consequent abandonment of notions like "adequation" and "correspondence" as part of a large-scale redescription of the human situation. Kolakowski is right that Mach's and Avenarius's criticisms of truth as correspondence to reality anticipated those of James and Dewey, but Dewey drew larger consequences from those criticisms than did his predecessors. Dewey thought that it was important to insist that, in Kolakowski's words, "the intended meaning of all our utterances is practical," even after he had agreed that, to use Kolakowski's example, sentences about human actions cannot replace sentences about rain. That is because he construed that claim about meaning not as a reductionist claim about the interchangability of sentences but as a way of saying that we invent and use words for the same reason we invent and use tools—to help ourselves get what we want.

However, one of the things we want—one of the things that gives us pleasure—is finding new and better things to want, new pleasures to have. We want to be richer, more complicated, more encompassing, more loving beings. Or some of us do, anyway: the lucky ones who have more money, more rest from toil, more chances to pause and smell the flowers. For such people, language often becomes a tool for self-transformation and for the special sort of happiness that self-transformation makes possible.

It may seem odd to think that one of the things we want is to become different from who we are. But for Dewey this was a plain empirical fact: a fact about how certain organisms started to behave after the struggle for survival became less fierce. At that point, cultural evolution acquired some of the transforming power which had previously been reserved to biological evolution. People began using language to become different sorts of people.

Dewey carried through, beyond the point reached by Mach and Avenarius, by suggesting that poetry and art, rather than God and Truth, are what lure us onwards and upwards. More generally, he took such products of the human imagination as temples, epics, and cities as evidence that human beings could, so to speak, invent carrots to put out in front of themselves. They could tempt themselves to forge ahead into uncharted territory. He thus linked philosophers' criticisms of Aristotelian notions of correspondence and of Cartesian notions of selfhood (criticisms which, as Kolakowski accurately says, antedated pragmatism by centuries) with romanticism and secularism. In saying that if we had poets we would not need God, or any surrogate for God, he was trying to further the Whitmanesque hopes of early twentieth-century America.

Dewey was continually reproached for being unable to answer questions of the sort Kolakowski raises: Useful for what? Useful by what criteria of utility? But he thought that these were bad questions, as bad as the questions True for whom? True by whose criteria? For pragmatists like Dewey, there are no answers to general, philosophical, criteriological questions, and there do not need to be. Only particular, regional, criteriological questions need answering. In the course of creating a well-defined, reasonably autonomous, social practice such as engineering or jurisprudence, we develop criteria as tools for regulating this practice. We appeal to these criteria when answering questions like "Is the bridge strong enough?" and "Is this against the law?" But the overall project of free societies—the project of occupying the democratic vistas—is not a well-defined social practice, any more than is writing or reading poems or falling in love. (These latter may of course be made into well-defined, criteria-governed practices, but then we get bad poems and unhappy marriages.)

Kolakowski speaks of "our inability to decide what, for whom, and on what time scale anything is useful or not." This seems to me rhetorical exaggeration. Such decisions are made all the time, and made rationally—that is to say, by the attainment of unforced, Habermasian consensus among informed inquirers, rather than by force or fraud. They are often made not by reference to any *criterion* but impressionistically—like decisions about which book to read, which church to worship in, which romantic advance to reject, or which wallpaper to select. But this does not mean that they are *arbitrary* decisions.

Decisions can only be called arbitrary if they fly in the face of recognized, previously formulated criteria. A judge acts arbitrarily if he or she says that something is a crime that his or her fellow judges are unable to find in the statutes. An engineer acts arbitrarily if he or she says "It will hold up" without bothering to apply the standard criteria for measuring tensile strength. But when I decide to propose to a woman who I hope may become my wife, I am neither applying criteria nor acting arbitrarily. When the American electorate votes against a candidate who favors racial desegregation or the Polish electorate votes against candidates who take their cues from the bishops, they are not applying criteria, but nor are they acting arbitrarily. They are making rational judgments, and in doing so they are transforming their country, and thereby themselves.

For Plato, and for all those who accept his distinctions between will and reason, or between passion and reason, the question Criterion-governed or arbitrary? is *always* appropriate: It can be raised about *any* distinction. So is the question, *Which* criteria? But Dewey did not accept Plato's distinctions between parts of the soul, since he thought that they incorporated precisely the distinction between corresponding to reality and practical utility that he wished to blur. Like me, he would not have been willing to accept Kolakowski's question "Why does the pragmatist think that these [utilitarian] criteria are good or better than any other?"

We pragmatists do not think that there are such things as "utilitarian criteria." There is just the practice of muddling through toward happiness as best we can.

Kolakowski may well regard what I have just been saying as one more version of the response that he says will not do, the response that "we do in fact apply utilitarian criteria, whether we know it or not." He thinks that this response will not do for three reasons, which I shall take up one by one.

His first reason is that "all philosophical doctrines, epistemological principles of old, religious beliefs, and traditional theories which the pragmatists want to kill might turn out to be good—since they exist—according to the pragmatists' own criteria." So they might. Kolakowski's implicit suggestion that since they existed, these old theories and beliefs must have been found useful by somebody sometime is quite right. Dewey very explicitly accepted this consequence and welcomed it. He thought that every evil was but a lesser good and that every rejected belief has some merits. It must have had *some* merits—have been found useful for somebody sometime—or else, as Kolakowski rightly suggests, it would never have existed.

These rejected candidates might turn out, on further examination, to be better than the ones for the sake of which they were rejected—just as old books sometimes turn out to be better than new ones, old tools better than new ones, old lovers better than new spouses, and so on. But this is not a reason for saying that we apply nonutilitarian criteria. We usually do not apply criteria at all. We just deliberate about various advantages and disadvantages. The question is not Are our criteria utilitarian? but rather Can we find any term less vacuous than "more useful beliefs" or "beliefs thought likely to produce greater happiness" to describe the aim we hope to achieve by such deliberation?

Pragmatists do not think we can, once the notion of correspondence to reality is given up. They have no special affection for the term "useful." They use it only as a handy rhetorical device for contrasting their view with the views of those who think that "the pursuit of truth" is a *non*vacuous way of describing the aim of such deliberation, one which contrasts with the pursuit of utility. Pragmatists think the claim "I want *truth*!" tells one nothing about the speaker, any more than does "I want *utility*!" Everybody wants truth, and everybody wants utility. The question is whether, for purposes of formulating a self-description at the level of generality at which philosophy traditionally works, the one vacuity serves better than the other. In the absence of correspondence to reality, the two are tied. Pragmatists think that one vacuity is better than two, since it avoids pseudo-contrasts.

I come now to Kolakowski's second reason for denying that the pragmatist can get away with saying that "we apply . . . utilitarian reasons, whether we know it or not," which is that "it would be difficult to prove the usefulness of many scientific theories or mathematical truths which enjoy the acceptance of scientists." In reply, I have little to say except that pragmatists try to extend the meaning of "utility" to include satisfaction of such desires as simplicity and elegance in the construction of systems of belief.

Is this extension of meaning just a trick, one which renders the notion of "utility" too vague to be of any use? Well, as I have said already, pragmatists do not think the term *is* of much use except as a rhetorical counterweight to traditional, equally vacuous terms, like "truth." The only point in talking about utility is to flesh out the picture of the human situation that emerges once one starts thinking of a language as a collection of tools.

Kolakowski's third reason for saying that pragmatists cannot make the move they want to make is that "one cannot reasonably argue that the intended meaning of all our utterances is, as a matter of fact, practical and that, for instance, when I say 'it rains', the intended meaning of this sentence is 'I better take an umbrella when I go out'." I have already referred to this point above. I quite agree that one cannot analyze sentences about rain into sentences about human actions, but that is because one cannot offer interesting "analyses" of sentences at all. The idea that philosophy might make progress through "linguistic analysis" was, as Wittgenstein and Quine have helped us see, a dead end. The pragmatists' claim that "the intended meaning of all our utterances is practical" is just another way of saying that we make utterances for the sake of getting what we want. That claim does not need to be backed up by finding necessary and sufficient conditions, phrased in terms of people and umbrellas, for sentences about rain.

Let me now return to my claim that pragmatists should be viewed as attempting neither to offer noncircular arguments, nor to satisfy criteria, nor to analyze meanings, but rather to transform human beings' sense of their situation. When I speak of self-transformation and of the invention of new self-descriptions, the principal example I have in mind is the transition from an atheistical to a religious self-image, or the converse. So it suits my purposes to focus on Kolakowski's claim that religious believers "believe in God because it is true that God exists."

Pragmatists do not see that this contrasts with "they believe in God because this belief is useful." One could get a genuine controversy going only if one expands the terms of argument—for example, if one side says "I can explain the phenomenon of religious belief by the causal connection between it and the existence of God, by the operation of Grace" and the other says "I can explain the same phenomenon by the causal connection between this belief and the believer's relation to his or her parents."

Pragmatists think that neither sort of explanation is of much use because nobody can produce independent evidence for the existence of either Grace or the unconscious role of the father figure—evidence which both sides would accept as adequate. That is why argument in these areas tends, in the end, to go round in circles, and it is one reason why "argument" is not the right word for the kind of thinking that produces self-transformation.

Given his view of language as a collection of tools, I think Kolakowski should agree that "they believe it because it is true" is never a useful explanation of anything. That phrase is no more helpful in clearing up the puzzlement felt by those who wonder how anybody could hold a belief which they do not than is the phrase "they believe it because they think that it is true" (an empty tautology).

Kolakowski is quite right that you cannot convince anybody of anything, much less of the existence of God, merely by pointing out the utility of the belief. But you cannot do so merely by pointing out its truth either. Persuading somebody to believe something is a matter of justifying it to him or her—showing how it fits in with his or her other beliefs better than the contradictory belief. Questions about whether we should believe something are never questions about the causes of beliefs nor about the utility of beliefs. They are always about the coherence of the belief with previously held beliefs. Once correspondence goes, that question about coherence is the only question about the belief's truth that we know how to discuss.

Kolakowski is also quite right in saying that it would be pointless to say Husserl and Dewey were playing different language games, or that the atheist and the religious believer are playing different language games. Such a remark would be pointless because it is obviously true and does not tell us what we want to know. We want to know which language game *we* should be playing. This is not a question we have criteria for answering. The only criterion in the area is something as vague as "what makes the most sense" or "what seems to add up" or "what seems to lead us in the direction we should like to go." That is because philosophical reflection is not a well-defined social practice like engineering or jurisprudence; it is a kind of discourse where the choice of means and the choice of ends (the choice of which language game to play and the choice of which life to lead) are hard to disentangle from one another.

Kolakowski is also right that it would be silly to say "Let's make a secret agreement not to play epistemological language-games," just as silly as an analogous recommendation about religious or atheistical language games is. But one can find oneself no longer wanting to play any of these three language games—not because one has applied a criterion, nor because one has made an arbitrary decision, but because one has found better things to do. At various times in recorded history, various language-games have, gradually and almost insensibly, ceased to be played and been replaced by others. There was rarely an argument for this change that could have been phrased in some noncircular way. Yet many of these changes are ones that have turned out to be useful, in the sense that they made us what, for better or worse, we are today.

It would also be silly to say that moves within a religious, or pragmatist, or Cartesian, or any other language game are "meaningless." Wittgenstein was right: Anything has a use, and therefore a meaning, if you give it a use. Anything can be a tool for some purpose. Charges of "meaninglessness" have gone out of fashion, even among the Anglophones, just as have attempts to give "linguistic analyses." We are well rid of both. Kolakowski is quite right to say that pragmatists should not invoke a distinction between talking about language games and talking about something else: between metalinguistic and first-order talk. If the pragmatist attempts to get any mileage out of this distinction, he will indeed, as Kolakowski says, find himself saddled with an "unpleasant and apparently insoluble conflict between two levels of language."

But giving up this distinction does not mean giving up the claim that 'useful' is preferable to 'true' when evaluating scientific theories, descriptions of the human situation, and the like. How does one evaluate this claim? Well, not by looking for a noncircular argument for it, nor by pointing out its counterintuitive consequences. Large-scale redescriptions of ourselves are always counterintuitive (since the intuitions were created by the description we are considering discarding). They cannot appeal to premises phrased in language which is neutral between that of old descriptions and that of the proposed new descriptions. There usually is no such language. We evaluate such claims in the same way as Europe evaluated the dispute between Aristotle and Galileo and that between the Church and Voltaire—in sloppy, messy ways to which questions about infinite regresses and circular arguments are irrelevant. These are the same sloppy, messy ways in which we make all the important decisions of our lives, either as communities or as individuals.

I entirely agree with Kolakowski that "pragmatism is as such as much a passing fashion as Platonism once was"—or at least that it may prove to be so. The relevant difference between pragmatism or Platonism on the one hand and Euclid's proof that there are infinitely many prime numbers on the other is that the former are controversial and the latter are not. That is not a matter of "status"—or the former being "cultural products" and the latter not—but of sociological fact. As it happens, nobody has come up with anything better than Euclid when it comes to the infinity of primes. Various people, including the pragmatists, think that they have come up with something better than Plato when it comes to a description of the human situation. Descriptions of the human situation, like systems of geometry and physical theories and religious creeds, are cultural products; but that is merely to say that they are tools that human beings have produced to serve (and occasionally change) their ends.

As I see it, Kolakowski's word "status" does not cohere with his agreement that languages are collections of tools. I should think that anybody who accepts this view would say that all statements have the same status: They are good or bad moves to make in pursuance of some end. So the difference between statements about torture and statements about knives and forks is not their different "status" but their different degrees of importance to the ends that we, the people who debate these statements, wish to achieve. For us, here and now, torture matters very much and table etiquette does not. Now imagine a really nasty culture, one in which the reverse is true. Is there a way to decide between the relative merits of those two cultures? Sure. It is the same messy, sloppy, nonargumentative, hit-or-miss way in which our culture emerged from earlier cultures.

Plato thought that there might be a non-messy, argumentative, noncircular way to make such decisions. Pragmatists cannot see that he found one, nor that the search for one, in later centuries, has proved profitable. So I do not think I can convert Kolakowski to pragmatism by any nice rigorous little deduction from his admission that languages are collections of tools. Nor is he likely to convert me away from pragmatism by arguments using terms like "status," words which strike me as obsolete tools. But perhaps our exchange, sloppy and messy as all such philosophical exchanges are, may help something to emerge.

NOTES

1. Hilary Putnam, *Realism with a Human Face* (Cambridge, Mass.: Harvard University Press, 1990), p. 28.

2. In this text, Professor Rorty offers his response to comments made by Jürgen Habermas to Rorty's "Relativism: Finding and Making." These comments have not been included in the present volume. The core of Habermas's arguments can be understood, however, from Rorty's replies, and many of them were included in Section IV of the final version of Habermas's "Coping with Contingencies: The Return of Historicism," included earlier in this volume. *Eds.*

Chapter 3

Philosophy and the Dilemmas of the Contemporary World

LESZEK KOLAKOWSKI: A REMARK ON OUR RELATIVE RELATIVISM

In the eyes of God everything is beautiful, good, and just, according to Heraclitus. It is not so in our eyes, of course. Heraclitus's assertion, however, does not imply a "relativistic" melancholy (God sees things one way, and human creatures another). We must assume that God knows better and thus that everything really is beautiful, good, and just and our common insight is not simply different, but plain wrong. It is conceivable—at any rate it is not logically inconsistent—that we do know that such is God's picture of the world and that it is accurate (for instance, God himself has told us so), but we are incapable of sharing it, except perhaps for some mystics who momentarily participate in the divine vision; but then, they have no means of conveying the same vision to others.

If we fail to perceive the beauty, and justice, and goodness of everything, but see instead a huge mass of ugliness and injustice, does it matter at all that we know or pretend to know that everything is indeed beautiful, and just, and good? I believe it does. It does not alter the content of our perceptions, it does not make our practical endeavors more efficient, but it may affect our attitude to the world. People who strongly believe—on the basis either of divine revelation, an untransmittable experience, or *a priori* reasoning, like Leibniz—that there is a good moral order in the universe and that ultimately everything is in the service of the good are not protected from ugliness, injustice, and suffering, but they are better able to absorb the adversities of their existence and to trust life, whatever happens. This does make a difference, even though their image of things cannot be reforged into an empirical hypothesis in conformity with the rules of scientific inquiry.

This difference is worth pondering when the question of truth is discussed. It is indeed hard to silence the traditional arguments that have been raised against both relativist and absolutist claims in the interpretation of human knowledge. The gist of the antirelativist argument is this: The relativist denies an everlasting and absolute standard of rationality. In the relativist's view, if we say that something is valid in our knowledge, we have to assume, implicitly or explicitly, that it is valid by reference to a particular civilization, historical conditions, human biological structure, or a linguistic game. But thereby, critics argue, relativists are entangled in a snare of their own making: They cannot escape the antinomy of the liar, for the general statement about the relativity of all knowledge falls prey to its own verdict and is as relative as any other; albeit conceivably true, it is, as it were, unutterable. One might seek refuge in remaking the epistemological statement into a normative rule; this would be a spurious solution, though, even if it removed the antinomy, as such a prescription would either appear arbitrary and therefore incredible or be justified by the very statement that has just been cast off.

The same applies, for that matter, to another kind of relativism, expressed in one of the most celebrated sentences of contemporary philosophy, Paul Feyerabend's "Anything goes." If anything is permissible, then all kinds of restrictive cognitive rules are equally permissible; in other words, the rule, "It is not the case that anything goes" also goes; thus we may say that if anything goes then it is not the case that anything goes. This sort of reckless permissiveness does not look very promising as a foundation for a theory of knowledge (to tolerate everything means to tolerate intolerance).

The Popperian variety of relativism might not fall victim to the self-reference paradox because it deals with empirical hypotheses and it does not pretend, if I understand it properly, to be itself an empirical hypothesis; but it implies other unpleasant consequences. If we assume that there will always be, after all eliminations, an amplitude of mutually incompatible explanations for the same empirical stuff, then it appears conceivable that our knowledge, accumulated in empirical hypotheses and laws, consists entirely of false statements and that this will be so forever. The distinction between truth and falsity is not abrogated, but it is of little use: While falsity can be established, truth cannot. No doubt rules of acceptability or admissibility can be devised, but not signs whereby the distinction between what is acceptable and what is true is established.

In all three variants of relativism the concept of truth as it is employed in everyday discourse is done away with. However, to discard any of those variants on logical or other grounds is not to reassert this very concept. Quite the contrary. The traditional argument of the ancient skeptics about the inescapable infinite regression that arises in the quest for criteria of truth still seems cogent.

The outcome of these well-known strictures is no less known: There is no point zero in the search for knowledge, no uncontaminated source from which certainty—real, unconditional, unimpeachable certainty—springs. Husserl's unflagging pleas for Truth—spelled with upper case—in the face of the relativist corruption of European civilization went largely unheeded, and this was not so because his arguments were necessarily faulty but rather because the prevailing cultural trends were going in another direction and eradicated, step by step, the belief in perennially valid standards of intellectual work, in the regulative ideal of *episteme,* and finally in the very usefulness of the concept of truth. These trends have reached their climax in our time, but we can trace them back with the benefit of hindsight to the very beginning of the Enlightenment, in the most encompassing sense of this lax expression.

Modern skepticism, we may guess, resulted from contact with other civilizations and affected, as we see in Montaigne, not only moral rules and customs, but all kinds of truth. This was, to be sure, before modern science emerged in the beginning of the seventeenth century, soon to be codified in a set of fairly distinct abstract rules of procedure. But the great thinker, the reputed pillar of modernity, who contributed to this codification and whose work could be seen at the start as a philosophical response to Galileo's physics was to become, unwillingly, a part of the skeptical conspiracy. Descartes's way to the restoration of certainty and the reality of our world of experience has been, of course, endlessly analyzed and commented on. But few have accepted it as a reliable method to establish trust in our cognitive prowess. His skeptical questioning worked more strongly and was repeatedly denounced as the main source of modern idealism.

It was the Enlightenment proper which, from various sides, cast more and more doubt on our proficiency in the search for truth as it had been traditionally defined. Hume, of course, became one of the main culprits when he ultimately reduced valid knowledge, apart from tautologies, to the content of particular perceptions, immobilized in their particularity, and everything beyond that to pragmatic values. So did Kant, at least in the popular perception of his work. Schopenhauer even argued that the Kantian distinction between phenomena and the thing-in-itself and his insistence on objects being inevitably co-created by transcendental forms of consciousness resulted in the conclusion that what we have to do with in the world of experience is the realm of dreams; we should suppose therefore that once Kant had been woken from his dogmatic slumbers by Hume, he would have realized that he was and still is living in a dream and that the world of experience is Maya, as the Vedic wisdom used to teach us.

This might have been an exaggerated interpretation, and Kant himself did not phrase his discovery in so many words, but when we look at great philosophers as cultural facts, what counts is less their genuine intentions than the way their thought acted upon and was perceived by the general educated audience. When he averred that his place was the "fertile depth of experience" he meant it, and his writings, sometimes opaque, were not designed to instil in his readers a feeling of tragic renunciation or a terror of the great Unknown. But his simplified message was that the world as it really is is beyond our reach; God's existence is unprovable; morality is severed from its religious roots. This was supposed to be "the withdrawal from immaturity, which we are ourselves guilty of," that is to say, the Enlightenment. To be sure, a school of Kantians did away altogether with the thing-in-itself as a fictitious construct and made of Kant the herald of the absolute sovereignty of Thought, but another school reduced his transcendental forms to psychological, species-related conditions of knowledge, thus reinforcing the relativistic side of his legacy.

Hegel took part in the conspiracy as well: again, less perhaps through his notoriously ambiguous intentions than through the way he was read. And it was fairly easy to perceive him as a historicist for whom all products of human thought, including philosophy, metaphysics, and religion, have to be seen as temporary tools of the great impersonal spirit in search of itself, and truth is time-bound and culture-related. Frequently, his philosophy was misread as an approval given by Reason to all of historical contingency.

A vigorous stimulus was given to relativist thinking by the philosophical elaboration of Darwinism. From a theory implying that the entire development of life is guided by one single factor—the mechanical elimination of the less well adapted—it was not implausible to conclude that the specifically human Reason we boast of, including its power of abstraction, is no more than an effective instrument of the adaptation of species to the changing environment and that this is the only framework of meaning we may reasonably attribute to it. In other words, that the proper measure whereby the validity of knowledge ought to and can be assured is its ability to predict and to control events in order to counteract the hostile contingency of nature in an efficient manner. The question of Reason and of Truth in the Platonic, Aristotelian, and even Cartesian sense became both empty and irrelevant to this task. This was what the empiricists of the late nineteenth century made explicit and consistently argued for.

Does the reduction of knowledge to a self-defense mechanism of the species, as suggested by philosophical Darwinism, fall prey to the antinomy of the liar? Not necessarily, if it is transformed into a prescription which can be applied to itself. It may be argued that in some interpretations the discovery of a theory of evolution is itself an instrument for improving the survival chances of the same species that contrived it; for instance, that it would be a good thing to slaughter its ill-adapted members, as suggested by some English lovers of mankind like H. G. Wells and George Bernard Shaw.

But philosophical Darwinians usually do not bother about this issue. The Darwinian theory is accepted as a scientific discovery, and the belief in its truth in the normal sense of this word is stealthily smuggled into reflections which deny the meaning of truth on the basis of the same theory.

Nietzsche, of course, was the noisiest voice of this cultural mutation, for all his contradictions. Quite often we spot a hidden despair looming up from behind his triumphal war cry over the dead bodies of God, Truth, Reason, and well-ordered universe. But the crucial, the poignant message could not be misheard: Nothing but pathetic wreckage has remained from the lofty platonic mirage of wisdom. We are no longer pilgrims doggedly and tirelessly striving toward this great treasure; the treasure does not exist—it is a figment of our hollow craving for the impossible. We live in an aimless chaos and try to assert our individual or collective will to expansion. Our philosophy, our religious search, and very often even art are but illusory veils we enclose ourselves with in order not to face the world as it truly is (never mind that there is no Truth).

But civilizations cannot survive in despair, not for long at any rate. A fairly optimistic interpretation and an efficient medicine has been found for what many people might have seen as a disaster: There is simply nothing disastrous in our reasonable renunciation of the chimera of Truth and Reason; this was just a ghoul that had been haunting our civilization for millennia and to some extent keeps haunting it. Why should we fall into despondency for no better reason than that we stopped stalking an animal from a fairy tale? Our knowledge has proved efficient and provides us with predictive power: What else do we need? If some of its parts turn out to be counterefficient or inefficient, they are cut off like dead twigs; what is acceptable is healthy and remains, and science itself devised good criteria of acceptability. People have been quarrelling, for instance, about "the existence of the world." But even assuming that we could define and grasp the meaning of such a bizarre query, it is the most futile and empty inquiry. Whether we decide that the world does or does not exist, nothing changes in our life, our perceptions, our practical business, our science. Let's throw away nonsensical worries which might have originated in sick minds.

Remarks of a similar kind can be made on most of the traditional problems of metaphysics and epistemology, apart from those that are of an empirical nature and belong to psychological or linguistic analysis rather than to epistemology proper in the Husserlian sense. Neither ordinary people nor scientists are tormented by the distinction between the coherence and correspondence theory of truth; they discriminate between the true and the false on the basis of common criteria of acceptability, the latter being regulated, in turn, by the question, What can we do with this truth?

Even physicists, who tell us that some descriptions of the phenomena they examine cannot be made without the observer or measuring devices being included in those descriptions, contributed to the belief that a pursuit of Truth which is utterly independent from the fact that we are engaged in this pursuit is vain; or perhaps the very notion of Truth is unintelligible. Einstein might have been dismayed by this perspective, but most were not.

Replacing criteria of truth with standards of acceptability thus conceived belongs to the program of moderate pragmatism, which makes metaphysics invalid but does not affect science, as the latter can operate and keep all its rigors without bothering about truth, except in the sense of acceptability. Immoderate, or extravagant pragmatism, which instead employs criteria of usefulness or even "happiness," may be left aside. Not because it is false—it is an arbitrary prescription anyway—but because it is impracticable to specify how such criteria are to be applied. Nobody knows how they should work, what and for whom, and in what time scale this or that is useful or produces more happiness, whatever this means. (Narcotics bring happiness for a while and misery in the long run. And who is wise enough to calculate the global amount of happiness, given the unpredictability of the effects of so many human endeavors?)

Extravagant pragmatism, needless to say, may not be seen as a compelling conclusion from the moderate one. However, the cultural impact of ideas does not operate according to logical rules. 'Efficiency' and 'usefulness' do not mean the same thing, but in cultural and psychological terms the road is short from the former to the latter. The claim that there is no truth in the Husserlian or Platonic sense does not logically entail that "anything goes," of course, but the route, albeit longer, is as possible as, for example, the route from the demand of freedom to anarchy. It goes without saying that I am for freedom and against anarchy, but there is nothing wrong in following the changes, sometimes unnoticeable, in the prevailing use of concepts, whereby the concepts eventually take on a meaning far remote from or even opposite to the original one. And, of course, it is not the sheer play on words which causes such displacements but cultural processes that occur in other areas of life—in the hierarchy of values, in customs, in science, in technology, in social stratification, in religious beliefs, in information systems—all of them acting interdependently, so that plausibly to isolate the precise impact that may be attributed to one of those forces is usually a matter of speculation.

From the austere, ascetic and lucid thinking of David Hume to the contemporary philosophy of hippies and flower children, often called postmodernity, the itinerary is convoluted and twisting but not untraceable. Still, it is not one step that causes the other but external energies, which are often hard to identify.

Despite the massive assault on universal, intellectual, and other standards, there are, fortunately, areas where standards still apply—notably in the sciences and especially in the so-called hard sciences, which, it seems, have not been affected by the irresponsible philosophy of butterflies. They can do without the idea of Husserlian Truth; they do not need explicitly to assert the eternal criteria of rationality, but they have elaborated some fairly precise rules of acceptability that work, all uncertainties and disputes notwithstanding. It is worse in the humanities, to be sure. But it would be an exaggeration to say that standards in historical studies have already been killed off by postmodernist propaganda. The latter is expressed more in programmatic appeals than in the actual practice of science, but signs of the invasion can already be detected. The "anything goes" creed has obviously won in the arts and made fairly strong advances in moral beliefs.

If we try to single out a particularly powerful cultural factor that has contributed to the progressing collapse of standards, we are tempted to think that it is the enormously accelerated increase in mobility, both spatial and social. Virtual extinction of village life in the developed areas of the world has destroyed the spiritual organization of space as a guarantor of stability and eroded the trust in tradition, which provided people with a number of basic moral norms and the belief in a meaning-giving order of things. This is not a new discovery. Many people have reflected on uprootedness as a distinctive mark of our time. The widespread feeling of insecurity or the absence of spiritual shelter could not fail to find ideological or philosophical expression. We shed the archaic "irrational" habits of mind not in order to enter the glorious kingdom of rationality but, on the contrary, to adopt new habits which dismiss the idea of rationality altogether.

There is no way back to the unsullied order of old, though; no nostalgia will reverse the course of change nor undo its alarming, perhaps calamitous, effects. But the need for certainty and Truth, to know the world as it verily is, is not a privilege of philosophers or their contrivance; it simply is human, and it is most unlikely that it will ever be extirpated. Various plagues of our civilization may be traced back to the loss of spiritual security. They include the widespread use of drugs, which give people the feeling of an illusory short-lived reconciliation with life; they also include the growth in violent criminality, a symptom of the refusal to find oneself a niche in an order which is experienced as no longer being an order. Religious fanaticism and the search for a pathetic satisfaction under the guidance of grotesque prophets belong here as well. For any unprejudiced mind, as Hegel says, Truth will remain always the great word that lets the heart beat more strongly. Quine, whose thinking may be seen as an expression of moderate pragmatism, says that both objects and God are cultural artifacts, but the former are superior in that they are more efficacious at predicting events. Assuming that Quine is right, it still holds true that the fictitiousness of the objects which science deals with is not something many people are bothered by or feel sad about, whereas once God is declared an artifact and people take this judgment for granted, their world is really changed, both intellectually and emotionally; the absence of God is really experienced, whereas human experience is not changed when people are told that objects are artifacts.

Science is usually trusted because it works, but on the other hand, it has contributed in another way to the same feeling of insecurity because it is unintelligible to most nonscientists, and parts of it, especially in quantum mechanics and cosmology, have been becoming increasingly counterintuitive.

Even on the assumption that truth is propositional—and this is a discretionary decree—rationalism remains another discretionary decree. The criteria of acceptability it set up are based on the prowess of truth thus discovered in predicting and controlling phenomena; this is to say, truth is conceived in terms of moderate pragmatism. This is culturally and historically explicable, but if taken unrestrictedly, dismisses the idea of Logos as an unattainable mirage, a capricious fancy. Critics who attacked this scientific or rather scientistic, instrumental reason—for example the Frankfurt School—and tried to safeguard the right and supremacy of Logos were not capable of precisely defining its scope of domination or the criteria it was supposed to employ in its discoveries. Consequently, their philosophy could be accused of being no more than a yearning after the Platonic or Hegelian paradise lost.

And then we are back at the beginning; since no compelling logical evidence can be provided either for the so-called instrumental reason or for the Logos of its critics, the ultimate justification of both lies in the realm of human needs. And nobody has the right to tell people: your needs are not genuine, I know better what you really need. The quest for knowledge that would satisfy our need for an all-embracing meaning of life and for valid, "true," moral rules, can be, of course, easily discarded as having nothing to do with truth. But so can the needs which stir or steer our curiosity when the point is to control our environment. If there is no unmediated truth, that is, a truth in which the one who knows and the thing known coincide, if our words are tools rather than a mirror or a carbon paper on which the universe leaves its unpolluted effigy, there seems to be no way to escape the rules of moderate pragmatism unless we admit that another route of knowledge is open in which words cannot be so deftly manipulated but rather suggest or draw us near a reality which is not empirical in the sense of common perception. Let us repeat: To claim a monopoly for the rules of scientism is an arbitrary verdict. Does the refusal of this claim amount to seeking gropingly for a lost treasure in the darkness? Perhaps. As Epicharmos said, everything precious is usually found at night.

We survive uneasily in a perplexing chaos, having forfeited our belief in infallible guideposts for thinking. It is a post-Enlightenment world in that it is Enlightenment turned against itself: the loss of Reason as a result of Reason's triumphant victory over the Unreason of the archaic mentality. And better not venture into "futurology," as the future does not exist by definition. Strong beliefs easily breed fanaticism; skepticism, or no beliefs, easily breed mental and moral paralysis.

ERNEST GELLNER: ENLIGHTENMENT—YES OR NO?

If I understand the terms of reference which were given for this debate, the question is something like this: Enlightenment—yes or no? Do we still accept the values and visions of the Enlightenment, or are we attracted by the countercurrent—which has various names, like postmodernism, relativism, and so on—which rejects, from various viewpoints, the outlook of the Enlightenment? And this, of course, is not only a general question of some interest in itself; it has local and topical relevance because, of course, what has happened to one half of Europe since the happy reunification into one intellectual world is a kind of moral–ideological vacuum, which is being rapidly and chaotically filled. Of course, one can argue about whether it needs to be filled, whether one needs deliberate theoretical engineering which will provide the furniture and the fittings, or whether one should wait; that in itself is arguable, but that is the context of the debate. I hope I have got it right.

I have been asked to moderate between the two positions, but I am, in a way, ill-suited for this, because a moderator ought to be in the middle or neutral, and I am not. I have very definite views on the topic of this debate, which makes it unsymmetrical, but I might as well come into the open about it. Whom could I deceive? Anyway, I do not wish to deceive anyone.

I am unsymmetrical in the sense that I am not fully clear about Professor Habermas's position. I have read his paper with care. It is very rich, very stimulating, very suggestive, there are very perceptive things in it, but I am not clear either, in the end, where he himself stands, nor am I fully clear about the German tradition which he describes: this oscillating flirtation between Platonism and absolutism on the one hand and periodic retreats to different kinds of relativism or historicism on the other. As I am not clear about his position, I fear and suspect that I will travesty him, and I will probably talk not with him but with a kind of stereotype and image of the German philosophical tradition. But I am sure he will correct me.

Let me briefly sketch how I see that tradition. Important German thinkers can be divided into the great noncheating ones and into the cheating ones (of course, language is prejudicial), and I like the ones who do not cheat. The two great summits of not cheating are Immanuel Kant and Max Weber. They were quite clear where they stood on this matter of the Enlightenment. In fact, it is arguable—and I have argued—that, in a sense, they are really one person: Immanuel Kant was a philosopher and Max Weber was a sociologist, but they are both really talking about the same thing, one of them describing it, supposedly, as the dilemma of humankind as such and the other one perceiving the historical context. But the dilemma they were describing was the same, and their reaction to it was very clear. The noncheating consisted of this: Stunning, genuine, and unique truth is available (for Kant, it is fairly straightforward: the truth had a name—Isaac Newton), and the price of this truth is that the old cozy moral cocoons, the underwriting of human and social values by the nature of things, are not available. On the one hand, we have knowledge, on the other hand, we have lost the cosmic underwriting. And Kant consoled himself for this situation by saying that, of course, the basis of value is only in ourselves—there is nothing else—but happily the selves we have are identical and they are rigid; the structure of the self regenerates values (it, of course, is not underwritten by anything outside, but it is the same machinery in all of us, in all rational beings, so it does not matter all that much). Weber added to this a number of things. Weber was a bit more ambivalent. It is neither good news nor bad news, but the new knowledge was here and it was historically rooted: He saw the historic specificity of the Kantian perception. Those are the good guys, the ones who state it as it is; anyway, when I say "as it is," I mean the way I think it is.

Then there are the cheating ones. The cheating ones, initially, of course, are the Hegelo-Marxist traditions, which say that there is a way out of this. The sharp chasm between 'is' and 'ought', between science and morality, which Kant described and Weber explained historically, is not that absolute. We may not have the old divine underwriting, but we have a historical process which is just as benign, so it is alright after all. And the historical process can be guaranteed to have a happy end. Kolakowski, in "A Remark on Our Relative Relativism," makes an en passant remark that Hegel is wrongly credited with the view that history is rational and reason reveals itself in history, but I do not see why "wrongly." He plainly says this, and I do not see why this is a travesty.

All this seems to be cheating. History is not cozily arranged for our benefit, and that tradition seems to be misguided. It was revived by the Frankfurt School and I do not know how closely Professor Habermas wishes to be identified with it. What I understand the Frankfurt School to be saying is this: First of all, it revived the kind of Hegelo-Marxist language and style of thinking; in fact it tended to obliterate the distinction between Hegel and Marx. It thought that apart from facts, which any old fool can gather and which do not mean anything, we have a thing called the critical method, which underneath the facts tells us the deeper facts and, incidently, tells us the value direction. They claimed, overtly or by implication, to possess some algorithm by which the perception of historical facts would also engender the solutions, and they despised people who were mere positivists, for merely sticking to the facts and not being in possession of this algorithm. Anyway, I would be interested to hear whether Professor Habermas accepts my, no doubt, caricature as being somewhere near the truth and how far he would dissociate himself from that position, with which many people associate him. There is a question mark hanging over this, but I may have got it wrong and I certainly may have got Professor Habermas wrong.

Now I turn to the other person I have been asked to comment on, Professor Rorty. Now there I am totally clear, both about what he is saying, that it is wrong, and why it is wrong. I mean it is terribly, terribly wrong. I have enjoyed debating with Professor Rorty on other occasions and this total disagreement, combined with—I hope and trust—personal cordialities, seems to me to bring out the best in academic life. I ought to say why he is wrong. To some extent, he has taken the wind out of my sails because he already said it himself in his answers to questions that have been raised about "Relativism: Finding and Making."[1] I think he half understands why he is wrong, but I do not think he understands it fully. Now Professor Rorty is, if you pardon the expression, an American. There is nothing wrong in that; Americans are human beings like everybody else. If Professor Rorty wanted to marry one of my daughters, I might object on the grounds of age or the fact that he is already married, but the fact that he is an American would not stand in his way, I assure you. I have no prejudices. But when it comes to philosophy, it is a different matter. There is a grave obstacle between Americans and perception of truth in philosophy, and the result of this obstacle is that they tend to become pragmatists. Pragmatism is precisely the expression of their disability in this field. Professor Rorty half sees it, because he has said, "Of course, two hundred years of stability and prosperity have a certain effect on one and make it easier to perceive this truth." No, I would say, it is not two hundred years but about three hundred years, and it makes them perceive not the truth but a terrible illusion. Now let me describe what the illusion is, and let me do this as simply as I possibly can.

Imagine a stormy sea in which a lot of people are on the verge of drowning. Some choking with the sea water in their throats, they are screaming for help (those who are still able to scream), and in the middle of this stormy sea there is one group of people in a very powerful, very stable motor boat, which is quite able to stand up to this weather and they are cutting through these waters, and some of them on this boat, who are called pragmatists, say, "Why are all these people making such a dreadful fuss? Look how calm we are. We're not screaming, we are at home in this world." Well, yes, indeed. If you are in a very fortunate position and you do not see the problem because the problem does not affect you, then, of course, you could take this complacent attitude of saying, "There is really nothing wrong with the ship of knowledge, the ship of knowledge is stable." Well, *theirs* is. The point is, as many people have stated (Santayana said it, Louis Hartz said it, as did many others), America was born modern. The problem of the great chasm between the Enlightenment and the ghastly *ancien régime* which preceded it does not affect them, because they never knew the *ancien régime*. They have some sort of vague notion about George III, but the whole of European history between the Pharaohs and George III is one big mess, which is interesting for tourism but otherwise does not terribly interest them. America was also born individualist, liberal, and rational. This is a slight exaggeration, but by and large the decencies of the post-Enlightenment version of the world is their birthright. They are extremely lucky. And they have managed to transmit it to the mass of migrants who have come there. But it means that the problem is invisible to them because the decencies are taken for granted.

There is no more comic document in the world than the preamble to the American Declaration of Independence: "These things we hold to be self-evident." My God, the things which they hold to be self-evident were unintelligible, blasphemous, heretical, or proscribed for the large majority of mankind. The notions that society is an association of individuals freely pursuing happiness as a right and choosing their ends and so on—all these things which are, indeed, the post-Enlightenment constitution and law of liberal societies—were there from the start.

Then comes the big news in the nineteenth century that nature does it too. The reason why Professor Rorty is so excited about Darwin is not so much that Darwin naturalized Man, that he put Man firmly within nature, but that nature is described as benign. Well, nature is not all that benign (in order for it to be benign, many of the participants have to be eliminated). But it is benign, according to Rorty's view, in that it leads to good end results. This means that the American blindness to history between the Neolithic Revolution and George III is fortified. You see this curve: Nature is upward moving; there is development toward ever better adaptation, ever the better control over nature. American history is indeed the same story. You assume that the bit in between more or less fits in, and that is pragmatism.

Well, the truth of the matter seems to me to be that, in fact, most of human history sees humankind stuck in social–cultural intellectual systems which inhibit knowledge. For most thinkers between the Neolithic and the Industrial Revolutions, the maintenance of order is given the first priority, and the advancement of knowledge and production is either secondary or simply not thought about because the option is not there. Therefore the way things were (as the Enlightenment saw it) under the *ancien régime*—namely, rule of thugs and humbugs, coercion and superstition dominating humanity—was not just an unfortunate error. It *was* a mistake of the Enlightenment to think that it was simply a stupidity which could be avoided. The political and intellectual arrangements of the *ancien régime* were the corollary of the human condition in a post-foraging but pre-industrial age. This was an inherently Malthusian situation, in which knowledge and resources do not grow but population does, and in which, consequently, preoccupation with coercion, status, and one's position in society trumps any concern with the growth of knowledge. So that is the kind of ghastly situation of pre-industrial Man, where knowledge is more or less impossible, and certainly advancement of knowledge is virtually impossible. It occasionally happens that this condition is escaped as a kind of miracle, as in Periclean Athens or Renaissance Italy, but it is a miracle which goes against the grain and is short-lived.

This brings me to the kind of philosophical superstructure of this situation. For Professor Rorty, the absolutism of the Enlightenment, the belief in a unique and available truth, is a kind of hangover of Greek metaphysics (and I think Professor Habermas also subscribes to this) and geometry and logic on the one hand and Biblical absolutism (the exclusiveness of a single deity, hence a single truth) on the other, and we ought to get rid of it. I would put it the other way around. The unitarian exclusiveness—Jehovah teaching humanity the law of excluded middle by excluding rival deities and therefore training humankind in the belief of the unique truth plus the unique determination of answers in Greek logic, geometry, and grammar—provided a kind of training for the sense of a unique truth which separates the post-Enlightenment world from the pre-Enlightenment world. This division has to be codified. I think it was greatly codified by Hume and Kant in the eighteenth century and recodified brilliantly by Popper in this century. This is where the truth seems to me to lie, whereas the counterwave of indulgent relativism is partly an affectation, partly danger.

This counterwave also has a social basis. As society gets richer and richer, the amount of time we spend, or have to spend, in serious work, in production, and in exploration of the world diminishes. There we have to behave ourselves according to the Enlightenment rules. The amount of time we spend in leisure goes up, and in the leisure zone, which is a kind of one big Disneyland, we do witness what might be called a Californiaization of culture, of which the late Paul Feyerabend made himself a prophet, where indeed anything goes and there are no constraints. So we are encouraged in this by our environment, which no longer has these Weberian qualities of requiring order and discipline (that goes for the work period); however, all the gadgets are made as intuitively accessible as possible, and people get used to the idea of a very user-friendly universe, in which you do what you fancy and it is alright. I think this counterculture is alright, but it might be very dangerous. So my vision is radically opposed to what I call pragmatist complacency. The reason the pragmatists, the Rortys and the Quines, can reject the *coupure*, that great Cartesian divide of Enlightenment, is precisely because they take the benefits of the post-Enlightenment world for granted since their culture never knew anything else. They do not know the danger, they were never near there. Admittedly, Professor Rorty is somewhat more complicated than my caricature of him would suggest because apart from the complacency there is also an interesting kind of messianic streak: On the one hand, everything is all right, but, on the other hand, in the future it might be even much more satisfactory, in a kind of dramatic, discontinuous way. Now that particular streak in his thought does not fit my caricature.

Let me finish by relating all of this to our distinctively topical context. The Enlightenment made a number of mistakes. One of them was thinking that the *ancien régime* was simply an error rather than being inherent in agrarian society. The other one is that they thought they could provide a new, alternative vision where falsehood would underwrite oppression and superstition and truth would underwrite an egalitarian, free, fraternal society, the new vision provided by the Encyclopaedists. That was a mistake. It was a mistake that was brought in and implemented with sociological sophistication by Marxism and that then collapsed. So there were, in fact, two decades ago (even one decade ago), two variants of post-Enlightenment societies in Europe: in the West, a messy, untidy compromise; in the East, a coherent, ideological monolith, which for various reasons did not work and then finally, dramatically, and in an unpredicted way collapsed. Now, of course, a question pertains to the people of the eastern part, suddenly deprived of a coherent vision, which at least provided an idiom for social life (even when people did not believe in it, they at least knew how to behave within it)—where are they to go? Well, I think this is precisely what is happening. Everyone is thinking about it. Do we emulate? And which bit of Western compromise? Do we emulate the codified but politically not underwritten vision of the Enlightenment? Do we emulate the counterculture? That is the question. Can it be done in a hurry? Can it be done with a purpose?

Finally, I have one other thing I would like to say. Professor Rorty mentioned "two Emersonian paths." One is American pragmatism and one is the European variant, which ends with people like Derrida and Foucault, and it is somehow implied that they are similar or of equal value. I do not agree—here I become pro-American for a change. It seems to me that the pragmatists, although mistaken, are intellectually gentlemen. One knows what they are saying, and they express themselves coherently; one knows where one disagrees. The philosophical prose of somebody like Quine is absolutely exemplary. I think the propositions are mistaken, but they are stated with a lucidity, so that one knows exactly where one is. The European variants are only partially critics of the Enlightenment; partly they are counterculture clowns. There is an element of deliberate obscurity and difficulty in their writing—it is fireworks. And this element in their work does, I think, preclude one from putting them on the same level. It is not an accident that Quine was a coauthor or cosignatory of a letter to *The Times of London* protesting against Derrida's honorary degree on the grounds of intellectual unworthiness.

RICHARD RORTY: THE NOTION OF RATIONALITY

Before turning to Professor Gellner's remarks, I shall first say something about the three questions which were initially put forward for discussion.

The question "Has the Enlightenment done more harm than good?" is one that I would translate into "Are the literary bohemias and the universities better than the churches as the homes of an intellectual and cultural elite?" That is, was the move of the priestly caste of Europe out of the churches and into the universities and artistic literary bohemia good for democracy? The answer seems clear—yes, it was. There are all kinds of historical, sociological reasons for thinking this.

On the second question, "Can a secular culture produce enough of a civic community to protect democratic society against collapse?" I think the answer is only if there is enough money around. That is, if there is economic expansion and the hope of further equality of opportunity for members of the society, then I think a civic community does not need the churches and it can get along with the poets and the scientists. For the same reasons as Jürgen Habermas gave, I suspect that the churches are going to stage a comeback as the money decreases. I shall regret both the shortage of money and the return of the churches.

On the third question, "Is the notion of 'rationality' of any use in articulating the nature of such a secular culture?" Habermas and I disagree. I think that the notions of unconditionality and universal validity run into trouble when you go from one set of truth candidates to another—that is, when you go from the propositions taken seriously before an intellectual revolution to those taken seriously after the revolution. I think it is hard to preserve the notions of unconditionality and universal validity across such changes in vocabulary.

I think the notion of "the force of the better argument," which Apel and Habermas have often used, needs to be supplemented and enlarged with some notion like "the force of the better vocabulary, the force of the better language." In order to blur the distinction between learning processes and world disclosure, I find it useful to avoid the notion of "the better" argument and replace it with that of "the argument that works best for a given audience." I find it simpler to stop using the notion of universal validity and to speak instead in terms of what can be justified to a given audience—to drop the heuristic fiction of a universal audience or an ideal audience. Some audiences, obviously, are morally and politically better than others. But I do not think that there are arguments which are intrinsically better or worse, independent of the quality of the audiences to which they are addressed.

So the notion of rationality that I still find useful does not have much to do with truth. It has more to do with notions like curiosity, persuasion, and tolerance. I think of these moral virtues as the virtues of a rich and secure culture, one which can afford to think of itself as engaged in an adventure—engaged in a project the outcome of which is unpredictable. In particular, such a culture may take up the project of changing its own moral identity. A society can hope to become a different society. Rather than confirming its own identity by systematic processes of exclusion, it can find its identity precisely in its willingness to enlarge its imagination and merge with other groups, other human possibilities, so as to form the barely imaginable, cosmopolitan society of the future. So I want to use the term "rationality" in a way which does not connect it with knowledge and truth but does connect it with the political and moral virtues of rich, tolerant societies and the superior sort of audiences which become possible in such societies.

Let me come now to the differences between Professor Gellner and myself. His view of America seems to me plausible, and it is certainly widely shared. But I think that most of the things he said about America were probably also said in the 5th century B.C. by the inhabitants of the poorer, jealous Greek city states about Athens. Athens was an imperial capital which seemed to its neighbors to be giving free rein to all kinds of "countercultural clowns," to use Gellner's term: for example, weirdos like Socrates and Euripides. The Athenians seemed to be saying, "In our city anything goes; we are so rich, so secure, we Athenians, that we can do anything; we don't need the tragic sense of life; we don't need a sense of abysses and chasms, because we in Athens have it so good." I can imagine the resentment, the suspicion, and the dislike that the rest of Greece must have felt. Yet that would have been a natural thing for Athenians to say, at least in the period between Marathon and the war with Sparta.

One may easily see America as a rich imperial capital, self-satisfied enough to tolerate all kinds of countercultural clowns, and lacking a sense of tragedy and abyss. But one might be able to inspire some sympathy for the Americans by emphasizing the parallel with Athens at the peak of its glory. If it had not been for those rich, boasting Athenians, we might never have envisaged many imaginative possibilities—some of which, a few millennia later, were actualized. I would like to think that even though America is certainly coming to the end of its imperial career, and may also be coming to the end of its time as a democracy, in its best days it may have offered a sense of new human possibilities.

When Nietzsche said in *The Birth of Tragedy* that Socrates and Euripides were no longer able to grasp what the pre-Socratic Greeks had realized, one can see a parallel with what Gellner says about the Americans not grasping what Kant, Weber, and Popper have grasped—the abyss that separates the true and the right. Augustine said that the virtues of the ancients were but splendid vices, and from the American point of view, the European tragic sense of life is but a splendid vice. The nobility of Kant and Weber is analogous, from an American point of view, to the nobility of Aeschylus, as looked back to by Euripides and Socrates.

It may seem extravagant to compare America with Athens, but, as Professor Gellner pointed out, that is the sort of *hubris* you have to expect from us Americans. Professor Gellner thinks of the American pragmatists as not as bad as the European breed of countercultural clowns—Heidegger and Derrida. The latter, he thinks, engage in deliberate obscurity. I disagree. I think these writers are called obscure only because new things sound strange to ears accustomed to older ways of speaking. I do not think Heidegger and Derrida are more deliberately obscure than Blake or Kierkegaard. Obscurity of this sort is a necessary first stage of cultural progress. So I differ from both Kolakowski and Gellner in my evaluation of these figures.

Let me now move on to a few things that Jürgen Habermas said about learning processes and world disclosure. I think it is certainly true that one can overdramatize and overromanticize the history of science. Since Kuhn, perhaps, we have done this more than we should have. I think a corrective to this is Kuhn's own first book, *The Copernican Revolution*. There he tells a detailed story of how it took a hundred years for Europe to switch itself over from the earlier vocabulary to the later vocabulary. What is interesting about that book is Kuhn's claim that there was no nice, clean "better argument" anywhere to be found. The century-long shift in opinion and vocabulary was very messy indeed. There was nothing you could call the application of a method or a set of criteria—nor even, I am inclined to say, much of a learning process. There was simply much ingenious muddling through. But when the century was over, the world had changed. People were living in a newly disclosed world.

The interaction of learning processes and world disclosure is just as complex as Habermas suggests. But I think that Freud might cause a difficulty for the Lakatosian pattern which he mentions. In the case of Newton there was, as Lakatos says, a status quo ante giving rise to anomalies. But it is not so clear that Freud was a heaven-sent solution to a set of antecedently recognized anomalies. Freud strikes me as an example of someone who brought about genuine change in our moral identities, in our deepest self-image, not because he proposed to clear up anomalies but simply because he thought of something that nobody had thought of before. People reacted to Freud not by saying, "Oh, *that's* why so-and-so happens" but rather, "Hey, maybe he's right: maybe I should start thinking about something I never thought about before—for example, the connection between conscience and cleanliness, between sexual repression and moral consciousness."

It seems to me harder to embed Freud in a previously recognized problematic than it is to embed Newton. I do not think that the situation in psychology that confronted Freud was comparable to the situation in physics that Newton confronted or the situation in biology that Darwin confronted. But I do not want to press this point very hard. I just want to say that sometimes you can easily integrate world disclosure with learning processes, but sometimes it is harder. Sometimes you get an epiphany—something that is not so much a response to an antecedent challenge as a sudden upsurge of the indescribably strange and wonderful. I think the age of the democratic revolutions was such a time, and the development of new attitudes toward sex—a development which we trace back to Freud—was another.

NOTE

1. See this volume, pp. 114–116.

APPENDIX I

Comments on the Habermas/Rorty Debate

MAREK J. SIEMEK

I should like to begin with some beautiful words which are to be found in Jürgen Habermas's essay, "Coping with Contingencies—The Return of Historicism": "While I am in political sympathy with the anti-Platonist iconoclasts, my philosophical sympathy is on the side of the custodians of reason in those periods when a justified critique of reason loses the awareness of the implications of its inevitable self-referentiality." I must say at the beginning that it is just Jürgen Habermas whom I personally have always held to be one of these custodians of reason in our not too reasonable times. That is why I liked his attempt to disclose the inevitable Platonist presuppositions at the bottom of even the most justified anti-Platonist critique of modern reason. And that is why I also liked very much the example he offered of Kant's critique of Hume's interpretation of causality. But I should like to raise one or two questions which concern the problem of the limits of possible and necessary coping with the contingencies of the new thinking—possibilities and necessities for Habermas, in particular—because I have understood his argument as precisely an attempt to cope with these contingencies.

My first question concerns Habermas's presentation of the difference between Dilthey and Heidegger and their two versions of historicism. I can see where one finds the weak points of Dilthey's attempt to provide philosophical foundations for historicism. I agree with the diagnosis that Dilthey's historicism made it impossible to formulate any truth claims or validity claims more generally. If authenticity of expression is the only available standard of evaluation, we have to face uneasy consequences at first for the cognitive character and status of truth-claiming enterprises. I agree with this definition and I agree also with the conclusion concerning Dilthey that Habermas formulates at the end of this part of his essay: "If there is no validity claim besides the context-dependent claim to authenticity, the enterprise of interpretation as a whole cannot count as a serious candidate for the promotion of knowledge and learning, not to mention science."

Habermas then discusses Heidegger, pointing out the difference—in favor of Heidegger, of course—that in Heidegger, with his new categories and his concept of the world, which replaced the traditional concept of subject, the world is no longer conceived "as the totality of facts or entities, but as the lived-in social space and historical time that form the horizons of our everyday practices."

This leads to my first question. Can one really interpret the early Heidegger in just this way? These formulations are very significant and very strong, I should say. Habermas refers to "the horizons of our everyday practices" as being formed by "lived-in social space and historical time"; but I doubt if any Heideggerian would agree that there is such an essential dimension of *Dasein* in *Being and Time* which could be called the *social* one (except in a negative sense, of course, as different forms of "inauthenticity," menacing the *Dasein* in the "public sphere" of "Man"). Moreover, is there really one which could be called a historical one? There is, of course, a kind of ontology of historicity, but is there a historicity itself in its real dimension?

It seems to me that Habermas's interpretation of Heidegger is very important but still unfinished. I'm not quite sure if it agrees with the real function and role of this philosophy, and this leads to my second question, a more general one.

Habermas suggests that the role of Heidegger's philosophy is that he had given back to interpretation the whole range of meanings and validity claims beyond self-expression and authenticity. A further assumption, moreover, is that Heidegger brought the concepts of reason, knowledge, and truth back to the center of philosophy—albeit, as Habermas himself writes, "in an oblique way." My question is, How much can (and ought) this oblique revival of reason, knowledge, and truth modify our general opinion of Heidegger? Habermas himself says that Heidegger renewed the Humboldtian conception of world disclosure. But the Humboldtian conception of world disclosure belongs inseparably to the tradition of classical German transcendental idealism. And Habermas himself writes about the great detranscendentalization of the world in Heidegger and in the whole contemporary culture.

My last question is this: Does Habermas—who is and always was a great representative of the best tradition of German transcendental philosophy—really see it as necessary to make this step backward and to take for granted what we hear today from all sides, that culture, science, philosophy, and thinking has been or ought to be detranscendentalized? I think Habermas has admitted too much to these detranscendentalizing tendencies of our time in this regard. He writes, at the beginning of the chapter about new historicism, concerning what we now call detranscendentalization: "The growing awareness that the contingencies of history had gained philosophical relevance increasingly undermined the extramundane status of an ahistorical and disembodied transcendental subject." Is the transcendental subject of Kant really extramundane? Is it really ahistorical and disembodied? These are the modern or postmodern myths.

Professor Habermas knows much better than I do that in Kant and Fichte above all, and perhaps in Hegel, it is just the business of the transcendental viewpoint to construct a perspective from which the subject is precisely no longer extramundane but quite intramundane; no longer ahistorical but essentially historicized; no longer disembodied but involved in his world of experience and life. One can read all this already in Fichte and Hegel, if not in Kant. And now, if Habermas formulates such a thesis, I am just asking how far we can go in this direction. Where is the limit of possible acceptance for us, for the people identifying themselves in some way with this tradition of transcendental philosophy? Habermas himself, in his formidable works from the 1970s and 1980s, has shown that this is not a dead tradition; that one can interpret transcendentalism in a quite modern way and in a way which is very important for understanding our contemporary problems, not just our philosophical ones.

To finish, do we really have to accept this new situation? Should we not try to break this great narrative, which tries to deconstruct all other narratives except itself? This is my question.

JOHN T. SANDERS

I am delighted to notice that the discussion seems to be shaping up as a celebration of the idea of *practice* as fundamentally necessary in the critical evaluation of all theoretical work, whether that theoretical work is given the honorific name of philosophy or not. I want my remarks and questions to be understood as being in that same generally pragmatic spirit.

At one point relatively late in his paper, Professor Habermas ascribed to Heidegger the idea that the task of philosophy consists primarily in critical self-reflection on the history of metaphysics. The practical or pragmatic upshot of this idea then seemed to be that such critical self-reflection can in turn—perhaps paradoxically—prepare us for ultimately transcending the conceptual limits of metaphysics as such (or, at least, avoiding metaphysics and its inherent limitations). Professor Habermas ascribes also a "deflationist" version of this Heideggerian position to Professor Rorty.

Now, however one evaluates the thought that we might be able to transcend or avoid the conceptual limits of metaphysics, I want to call attention to a possible ambiguity involved in the very idea of such a thing. On the one hand, such transcendence might (at least in principle) be meant to indicate an avoidance of all contingent constraints on thought. But that would be exactly like asking for a point of view from which we could see things which nevertheless avoids all contingent constraints on vision, or for a way of describing things that avoids all the linguistic and other constraints on description. I am sure that this interpretation is not what either Heidegger or Rorty had in mind, since I am sure, given their overall positions, that they would agree with me in insisting that such unconstrained viewing, describing, and thinking are not only impossible, but quite incoherent. We cannot transcend or avoid the constraints and limitations of metaphysics if what we mean is transcending all the constraints that are inherent in thinking itself. *This* kind of transcending is no mere paradox.

On the other hand, what we can do—and perhaps this is what really *may* be recommended by Heidegger and/or Rorty—is to transcend or avoid whatever constraints that there have been up until now in our own points of view. Our rehearsal of the history of metaphysics can help us to learn where we are limited; it can help educate us. Such education might not come easily, of course. Our egos might make it difficult for us to see our mistakes and limitations; we may instead be too powerfully impressed with our own ingenuity. But there is definitely a chance that critical review of the history of metaphysics might indeed educate us and may even help to cultivate other ways of looking at things.

But rather than preparing us for transcending or otherwise avoiding the conceptual limits of metaphysics as such, it seems more reasonable—and more accurate—to think of this undertaking as preparing us for making our own contributions to that very history. Rather than getting away from metaphysics, perhaps what we can do—through critical self-reflection concerning the history of metaphysics, among other things—is to improve, along some path, our own metaphysics. I rather suspect that neither Habermas nor Rorty would wish to put the matter like this, but why not?

And now, still in the same generally pragmatic spirit which appears to be animating the entire discussion, I must say something about Professor Rorty's reactions to Professor Habermas's paper. I confess that I am still not sure I understand Rorty's hostility to ideals such as the ideal of truth. My complaint is not new, perhaps, but it still cries out for a clear response. Such ideals as the ideal of truth—and ideals like those of reason and morality surely stand and fall with the ideal of truth—seem plainly to have an enormous pragmatic value. They lure us out of our too-constrained, too-limited ethnocentric or idiosyncratic frames of reference. It is always possible, of course, that such ideals may be abused; they have frequently been deployed, in particular, as clubs used to beat down views and modes of behavior that are threatening or otherwise disliked.

But they need not be abused. Their proven and potential value is quite extraordinary. They offer us standards which pay explicit respect to the principle that the criteria we use for evaluating ideas and modes of behavior should be *non*ethnocentric and *non*idiosyncratic. They offer us standards that we can appeal to in luring ourselves or others to step outside of our relatively narrow present points of view here and now and toward a broader perspective that can serve us better tomorrow and elsewhere.

The *pragmatic* problem with embracing and encouraging too much relativism seems to be perfectly clear. If man is the measure of all things—if that really is true—then when my neighbor takes a position that seems to me to be deeply threatening, there is really nothing short of blows and weapons that I can resort to in trying to ease the threat. The regulative ideals of reason, truth, and morality serve to moderate attempts to persuade that could too easily otherwise resort to weaponry.

Professor Rorty, like Professor Habermas, has always insisted on the crucial importance of finding ways in which people can learn to moderate their attempts to persuade, especially in threatening situations. But I do not see anything in the doctrine that man is the measure of all things—in relativism—that can accomplish this. Indeed it strikes me that relativism is a profoundly *dangerous* doctrine in a world in which the differences between people seem to be getting more and more shrill.

So I ask Professor Rorty this: What is there, in his own reformist program for philosophy or for theoretical thinking, that can fulfill the extraordinarily important regulative ends that the ideals of reason, truth, and morality traditionally have served?

ANDRZEJ WALICKI

My comment will be very brief and it will mostly concern what Professor Rorty has said in his response to Professor Habermas; but it will also concern Professor Habermas's essay. In particular, I would like to point out a certain contextual difference between philosophy in a democratic society like the United States and philosophy in post-Communist countries. I think that this should be taken into account in order to understand the possibilities of dialogue which are created by this difference.

I believe Professor Rorty has suggested that a democratic society should avoid foundationalism because it is not pragmatically useful and proper for such a society to put such notions as truth, transcendental truth, or reason in the center of its culture. All right.

However, whether we like it, we must realize that in post-Communist societies the situation is diametrically different. People are afraid that without objective universal standards it is much easier to become manipulated, duped, and enslaved. A contextual, situational, antitranscendental conception of truth is, in such conditions, suspect, as it were, because it is seen as strangely similar to the dialectical sophistries of Marxism, with which people have had very bad experiences in the past.

In the 1950s, the situation was different, because by then the main threat to freedom was Communist fundamentalism—Communist dogmatism—claiming a monopoly on truth. In such a situation, historicization and detranscendentalization of truth was very attractive because of its liberating effect. This explains the interest of some philosophers of that time—mostly Marxist revisionists like Leszek Kolakowski and people going beyond Marxist revisionism at that time to different versions of historicism and praxis-oriented historical interpretations of Marxism (like Antonio Gramsci's historicist and praxis-oriented interpretation of Marxism, like the sociology of knowledge, and so on). And, of course, it is by then that Leszek Kolakowski wrote his very well known refutation of the classical definition of truth.

But the erosion and disappearance of dogmatic Marxism and Communist fundamentalism, which already took place in the 1960s, completely changed this situation, creating instead a very visible demand for epistemological and moral certainty. The demand for such certainty makes the situation not very congenial to the detranscendentalization of truth and similar notions. Many philosophers in Poland argue that we need Christian values, absolute values, or some form of foundations. Such views seem to prevail in the general climate of opinion in Poland, and this is historically explicable.

STEFAN MORAWSKI

It does not make sense to intervene between the positions taken by Professors Habermas and Rorty. One has to agree with the conclusion of the latter that we must inevitably choose either the theoretical conviction that our species and society are a lucky accident which occurred and goes on within the context of manifold, changing natural and cultural determinants or the conception of immanent teleology, which relates to some kind of essences. Let me note that such a conclusion concerning the controversy remains paradoxically inconclusive because there is no end to it. Maybe the only sound result of this encounter would be to open the doors for other propositions which similarly demand approval or rejection. I find the inconclusiveness a normal (and topical) feature of all philosophical discussions bordering on metaphilosophy. One knows lucidly that there are many possible solutions of how to make sense of the world and, primarily, of our existence: They compete one with another, they compel us to join this or that stance or look for our own. There is no escape from this *pari de la pensée* (I deliberately paraphrase Pascal to remind us that the choice is always ours but the things around and beyond us challenge our options). As far as my philosophizing was and is carried out, Professor Habermas's views are much closer to mine. Actually, I would be inclined to share them, with two—most probably unimportant—reservations.

First, I do not understand what reasons there are to deny the universalistic claims pertaining, as I assume, equally to Logos and mythos. Professor Habermas seems to take into account only the power of *Vernunft*. But since he dwells on Heidegger, it is worth remembering that the return to ontology (in contradistinction to the Diltheyan expressive symbolics grounded on the subject) was at the same time an attempt to transcend Logos toward the archaic sources of *Dasein* and a language which is seminally poetical. I would add that, all together, the modern attention paid to what is individual, unique, fluid, and so on revived mythos versus Logos, but not at the price of abandoning transcendental and universally relevant meaning and value.

My second qualification concerns Dilthey. I agree that the emphasis he laid on the multiple interpretations of the world was at odds with his claim to promote *Geisteswissenschaften* as firm knowledge. However, I see in Diltheyan pluralism a good starting point for rendering any kind of philosophy (or philosophizing) as one of many open choices. I would only improve his scheme by warning against separation of the interpretive endeavor of building a *Weltbild* from cognitive components and against the reduction of the typology to three possible worldviews. In other words, the authenticity of experience, even the richest and deepest, cannot be a criterion which provides anything more than a private interpretation of being and ourselves. Nonetheless, Dilthey gives us a key to the multiple, cognitively different philosophies which legitimize the ultimate indeterminacy of each determinate choice.

I have to stress at this point that the above kind of metareflection does not amount to what Professor Rorty presents. Now I would like to address his conception. I have already had a chance to participate in a dispute focused on Professor Rorty's views (see "Ruch Filozoficzny," 2, 1993, in English). As some of his answers to my questions did not quite satisfy my curiosity and eliminate my doubts, I willingly take advantage of the present opportunity to reenter the discussion, the more so because Professor Rorty, while synthesizing and clarifying his position, has compelled me to rethink my previous reading of his works. I still have trouble, however, following his approach.

Professor Rorty maintains that, being no enemy of reason and common sense, he criticizes, with his neopragmatist colleagues, some antiquated philosophical dogmas. Such criticism was and is practiced by many other thinkers far from neopragmatism. Hence, what matters in this case is the most radical, antimetaphysical orientation involving a specific language, namely one deprived of any claims to declaring what is true and false. Professor Rorty speaks of a narrative without any pretensions to reveal the essence (the very nature) of being, cognition, ethics, and so on. He repeatedly offers the view that there is no distinction between making and finding, discovery and invention, reality and appearance, objectivity and subjectivity. He invites us to a conversation which should avoid the pitfalls of Platonism–Hegelianism; that is, of surrendering blindly to the heritage of Western philosophy, which revolves around some alleged figments of the mind.

Is Professor Rorty's vocabulary and discourse really free of these bonds when he argues that his position is more sound—more justified—than that of his "antirelativist" opponents? I contend that his reasoning finally refers to the manifestly laid down (or cryptic) principles which should be assented to as stronger than these of his polemicists. His arguments do not stop at refusing to talk in a special way. His talk, albeit different and sharply critical of "the metaphysics of presence," does not indeed leave the traditional philosophical territory. I mean by this that without reintroducing the concept of truth, Professor Rorty's arguments drive home an idea of cognitive validity, the frame of reference of which is the rivalry between—to apply his terms—dualists and antidualists. This duel would be senseless if antidualism was not another approach to the same question which links Sartre to Derrida, hermeneuticians to James, Putnam to epistemological realists, and all of them to Kant. Briefly speaking, Professor Rorty's self-analysis is no loose narrative but a highly professional discourse trying to refute a selected heritage for the sake of proving the superiority of his antimetaphysics on familiar philosophical ground.

Professor Rorty's answer to the above objection is that the only affinities between the thinkers mentioned here are founded on a redescription (an equivalent to Derrida's deconstruction) of the problematics with which the family of so-called philosophers was always busy. We learn, however, that the cultural activity called philosophy can hardly be distinguished from other activities called scientific, artistic, political, and so on. No method and no specific discourse, we are told, will do to serve as the peculiar constituent of philosophizing. There is, moreover, no privileged place of philosophy in the domain of culture. Philosophizing is but one of many problem-solvings. One would like then to ask why these specific problems are called philosophical by Professor Rorty. He is prone, as I understand him, to opt out of and thus get rid of the bequeathed barren speculations ("tramping round and round the same dialectical circles"). If so, why not leave philosophy entirely? And why spend precious mental energy on paraphilosophizing (digging into the heap of old stubbornly reiterated mistakes) instead of being occupied with another mode of problem solving which needs no excuses? If we are encouraged to throw away the ladder which our ancestors used for their idiosyncratic purposes and to change the vocabulary (that means to put entirely different questions), why should there be any interest in this bygone stuff? My questions do address what I see as Professor Rorty's inconsistency, but my aim is not to pin them down as something wrong (inconsistencies belong to all serious philosophizing and are most often quite fertile).

My conjecture is that, fortunately, Professor Rorty, although changing the questions (e.g., instead of asking about the truth and the moral imperative, he asks about human happiness), is still rooted in metaphysics and splendidly continues the history of philosophical reflection. Why do I suspect this? Because his problematic touches upon the fundamentals of our existence (even by denying the intrinsic nature of reality) and holds us captive within the limits of reasoning which cannot be identified with literary narratives, political rhetorics, or scientific explanations.

The very beginning of his pragmatist credo—that is, the Darwinian premise (human beings as animals coping with the environment, employing words as tools), his dismissing of the Cartesian Theater of representation (correspondence between thought and reality outside of us), his emphasis on our "sentential attitudes," the goal of which is to behave here and there in the optimal way—all this proves beyond any doubt that Professor Rorty's antimetaphysics is actually another version of the very metaphysics so fiercely attacked by him. Empirical data involving the most efficient accomplishment of given tasks are by no means sufficient to construct the naturalistic *Weltbild* of Professor Rorty. His premise, according to which we should bind all our desires and beliefs to purposes which may be more or less adequately fulfilled within favorable or adverse circumstances, is not an empirical observation; it is a basic statement pertinent to the human condition. Thus it is one of those pressing issues which are beyond factual. Similar things may be said about his other major assumptions. For instance, he assumes that the truth of any belief consists in a better habit of acting, which in turn boils down to always trying to gain. From my perspective, this is sheer metaphysics, no different in its character (although not in its quality) from one based on the lessons of Scripture.

Let me tentatively and self-confidently assume that my remarks hit the mark. This brings me to further detailed counterarguments. With astonishment I read that although bank accounts are made and giraffes are found there is in fact no cogency to discriminate between them because, as Professor Rorty states, both suit our needs and interests. One can hardly abide by this statement because it lays bare that either (1) our attitude to any thing (any person) outside is confused with what that thing (or person) is in itself, or (2) the author wants simply to cancel this distinction as not worth pondering. In the first case—taking into consideration that Professor Rorty acknowledges the causal independence of giraffes from humans—such blurring of demarcation lines does not seem plausible or recommendable; in the second, if it is mere wordplay, it is obviously an arbitrary stratagem, because theorizing is incorporated into practical activity. Briefly stated, doing should absorb knowing. Why and on which grounds? I deem that it is not pointless to inquire what is the structure of atoms and which are the characteristic traits of species which comprise giraffes. If we even accept the pragmatist principal idea that descriptions are always relative to purpose, *cognitive* purpose would still have a special status. Examining the case of the giraffe therefore cannot be put on the same footing as investing money in the bank.

Professor Rorty is ready to leave the quarrels between foundationalists and antifoundationalists to the high-brows, but he attaches great importance to moral choices because they concern everybody. I go along with this hierarchy of values, and I would like to underline at this juncture that the accusations against Professor Rorty of being antidemocratic or denunciations of him as being oblivious to humankind's lot and state are either misunderstandings or mischievous gossip. Nonetheless, I wonder how it is feasible to throw out the concept of Reason (in its Enlightenment or other version) and still insist on distinguishing good from evil. If moral struggles continuous with the struggle for existence imply that what is just is nothing but the expedient and the prudent in a given situation, how can one at the same time defend the view that ethics should be founded on diminishing human suffering (first of all, violence and cruelty) as well as increasing human equality? In extreme circumstances, being expedient can mean precisely more suffering (say, giving up the fight with an enemy, conforming to his or her rules in order to survive). Why should expediency, which is based on gaining the upper hand over things and people, result in fostering human equality? This is a conundrum. No close substantial or logical association between these two "moral" categories can be devised.

I am eager to agree with Professor Rorty when he argues that to be moral one must not look for a supernatural court of law. But I am far from being persuaded by his renunciation of a legitimizing principle lurking behind every right action, a principle which is supposed to be of universal relevance. We live with different rules of what is just or unjust (from culture to culture, from one age and space to another age and space, from one individual to another), and this state of moral chaos threatens us with nihilism.

Professor Rorty does not subscribe to nihilism any more than I do, but as proper ethical therapy against both radical relativism and absolutism he recommends a search for the best and most rational solution, all factors considered, in such and such a situation. 'Most rational' and 'best' amounts in this context to 'most expedient'. Is this really good medicine? Does it meet Professor Rorty's other moral requirements? For example, he would like to see humankind as a family of brothers and sisters, in solidarity with one another, never doing unto others what they would not tolerate in regard to themselves. I conceive a bridge between these two statements to be possible only if one takes seriously the resemblance between what should be practiced and understood as just action and the Christian doctrine or its secularized, Kantian theorem. In another articulation, I wonder if the situationist (instantaneous) ethics—which seems to be self-contradictory because its criteria of value are constantly changeable and its "catechism" consists in boundless permissivism—will yield room to a genuinely principled ethics.

It is true that people are happy in diverse ways and the rule of happiness is similar to the rule of expediency or a consequence of it. But such axioms as human equality and freedom cannot be reduced to contingent, blatantly adaptive (here and now) attitudes and appreciations. There is a necessity to assume some transcendental *quod iuris*, something which refers to the common core of all humans who, even if they are the greatest sinners, would agree about the nature of sin. Is it not symptomatic that Lyotard and Bauman, when dwelling on ethical issues, ultimately look for support in Levinas's theological metaphysics, in the fathomless, inscrutable, and mysterious confidence which God's omnipresence imposes upon us and demand that we become hostages of the Bretheren's Face? Lyotard struggled with his pagan "commandments" derived from sophists which lead, as he feared, to the formula "everything goes." Already in *Au juste* (1979) he drew on Kant to rephrase the formal idiom of the categorical imperative so that the deontic law could be beyond circumstantial and stable but without transcendental involvements. This did not work, but the endeavor was continued in *Le différend* (1984) by means of bringing the ethical issue to Kant's *Critique of Judgment*, to the concept of *sensus communis*, which is obligatory thanks to reflexive judgment but cut off the epistemological stronghold.

In recent writings, Lyotard moved from Kant to Levinas and in order to avoid "theological" engagement speaks of something like ineffable moral instinct. This recalls the eighteenth-century English idea of a moral sense which is intrinsic to the human condition. I find an analogous move in Bauman's turn from morality without ethics to what he, as far as my understanding of postmodernism goes, mistakenly defines as postmodern ethics. Ethics it certainly is because he leaves behind the situationist approach bearing upon the rule of instantaneous expediency and, in fact, accepts a metaphysical, irrational principle of being moral before being social. I am, by the way—with Professor Rorty as well as with Lyotard and Bauman—against a codified ethics if it consists in scholastically fixed recipes dictating how to behave in all particular situations and in claims that these recipes are set once and for all. Such ethics simply kills morality, which can be alive only when challenged by complex conflict-ridden choices. Yet I mean by "code" something else, that is, the fundamental moral axioms which have to be concretized by each individual in her or his options and actions. I contend that Professor Rorty when appealing ultimately to nonviolence and noncruelty—that means to solidarity with all people (beyond any given ethnos, which more often than not happens to be xenophobic and within which therefore the shared beliefs turn into intolerance or merely hate)—in fact transcends the domain of expediency in the direction of a principled ethics of universal relevance.

One must inquire further whether ethics can dispense with truth, for I would ask on which grounds it is legitimate to approve of nonviolence and noncruelty as the highest (principal) values. Human dignity, the inviolability of human life, warm benevolence, or love to our brethren have to be confirmed as ontological foundations. If I am right, is this not metaphysics, even if its inventory is naturalistic, Darwinian, and pragmatist?

The theoretical frameworks of Professors Habermas and Rorty, as stated at the outset of my commentary, are opposite. Since one has to choose, I endorse the viewpoint of the former (although this does not mean that I espouse all his philosophy). But there is a possibility of discussing these opposite assumptions and conclusions on the territory of the same discourse. Professor Rorty—in counterdistinction to Lyotard's idea of *dissensus*—provides the opportunity of negotiating whether the question of truth and reality outside of our habits of action is indispensable or if instead we should do without it. That is why I consider him to be a philosopher, a great critical master who sets our minds on the alert. I take his side when he objects against treating the philosophers as priests who know everything and for good. Nevertheless, his own philosophizing informs us that this kind of problem solving has its specific, privileged merits. Namely, it spells out and can awaken the most lucid self-consciousness of who we are and which are the limits of our cognitive and ethical potentials. The culture would be much poorer and weaker without philosophizing, even though philosophizing must remain inconclusive.

But let me avow again that Professor Habermas's stance and questions are much more like mine than are those of his partner. There is nothing astounding in this inclination of mine when one considers a confrontation of the philosophical cultures of Germany, Poland, and the United States. But I would go beyond the cultural vicinity. My attraction to Professor Habermas's philosophizing has a deep impulse in a desire to defend what is threatened. Professor Rorty does not mind losing "philo-sophia." For me this loss would mean not liberated but truncated thinking.

Appendix II

Comments on Richard Rorty, "Relativism: Finding and Making"

LESZEK KUZNICKI

My few remarks should be considered as made not by a philosopher but by a biologist who during the last forty years, in addition to experimental research, has been dealing also, from time to time, with problems of the development of notions in the biological sciences, with questions about the structure of scientific revolutions, and with the possibilities offered by adopting reductionism to explain biological phenomena.

The substantial majority of present-day researchers, particularly those engaged in experimental research, have a rather poor or superficial acquaintance with contemporary problems of philosophical thought. Once they get acquainted with the foundations of pragmatism, however, and with historical relativism in particular of the kind advanced by Thomas Kuhn, they accept these doctrines as being very close to or even concurrent with their own concepts of the structure of the development of science. Notions used by experimenters, irrespective of whether they are biologists, chemists, or physicists, are always for them instruments of effective action. It is a pragmatic approach of this kind that is generally practiced, in large part completely unconsciously, by the majority of scientists. As a consequence, that which we understand as a truth will be only a general designation for the subsequent processes of verification and will shift gradually like a horizon in line with the advancement of knowledge.

Frankly speaking, arguments and quarrels between Platonists and anti-Platonists and Kantians and anti-Kantians are unintelligible—or at least not interesting—to the majority of researchers. The tradition of American pragmatism, therefore, which attempts to break the barriers dividing the physical and natural sciences on one side and philosophy on the other, seems generally to be closer to their way of looking at things. Here, however, we encounter an obstacle. Some branches of biology and some methods of explanation characteristic of the biological sciences cannot be brought within the framework of reductionism. The point is that Darwinism itself—or rather the theory of natural selection—applies separate notions, that is, "compositional" notions. The biological sciences taken as a whole, therefore, are not methodologically coherent. Molecular biology is methodologically identical with the physical sciences, whereas ecology more closely resembles sociology.

Biological classification, a typical empirical undertaking, particularly as it involves the denomination of individual species, has developed continually. In contrast, the semantic notion of "species," as part of a theoretical system explaining the classification procedures, has developed discontinuously from Aristotle until today. There is no coherence. This example speaks in behalf of historical relativism.

Kuhn's simple scheme was not confirmed in the development of the most general theory of life, the theory of evolution. Darwin's theory of natural selection, it is true, undoubtedly had all the traits of a paradigm; but the later development of evolutionism departs from the scheme proposed by Kuhn.

Twenty years after the publication of *On the Origin of Species*, evolutionism found itself in a crisis that lasted for over half a century (during which time many facts and partial theories were developed). After the crisis, there was no new paradigm.The improved theory of natural selection was called neo-Darwinism, or the synthetic theory. After approximately thirty years of the domination of neo-Darwinism (1940–1970), a new crisis emerged in connection with the discovery of the role of neutral mutations and punctualism as mechanisms of innovation. A state of crisis, without a dominating theory, has now lasted for twenty years.

For contemporary scientists, philosophy matters only insofar as it enables them to discover effective strategies of cognition and implementation of the rules of nature. The future, therefore, belongs to pragmatism.

ANDRZEJ SZAHAJ

I would like to say something about the political dimensions of the theories of Professors Habermas and Rorty, and I would like to begin with the declaration that I accept most of Richard Rorty's philosophical and political views. I should like, however, to formulate a few doubts as to some elements of the views in question.

The most important question for me is this: Should not a real pragmatist take the steps needed to be genuinely effective? The point is that if we take utility as the main criterion of the value of beliefs, we must ask ourselves which kind of rhetorical appeals to which set of beliefs will be the most efficient in a given situation. Let us say we want to remove a concrete evil from our social life. What if in a given local situation—because of some historical and cultural contingencies—only an appeal to a certain set of values and beliefs, treated by the citizens as absolutist ones, can effectively mobilize and motivate them to act against that evil? Should the pragmatist accept the situation, and appeal to these values and beliefs? Or should the pragmatist rather try to persuade such citizens that the values in question are only the result of particular historical and cultural phenomena and should not be treated in this absolutist way? Which part of the pragmatist narrative should prevail in this situation—the antifoundational part or the proeffective part?

In Poland, many years ago, in a very specific political situation, a thesis about the necessity of self-limited revolution was formulated. I think that from time to time one could, *per analogiam*, speak fruitfully about a self-limited pragmatist revolution against prevailing metaphysical, foundational ways of thinking. It seems that sometimes such a self-limited approach could be very helpful in reaching certain pragmatist goals, especially in the political dimension of social life.

I also agree that description of moral choice is "always a matter of compromise between competing goods rather than . . . a choice between the absolutely right and the absolutely wrong." In addition, however, I think that pragmatists should accept the possibility that sometimes an appeal to "the absolutely right against the absolutely wrong" may be the most efficient way of removing social injustice and building a sense of solidarity among people suffering pain and humiliation. I agree that "what matters for pragmatists is devising ways of diminishing human suffering and increasing human equality, increasing the ability of all human children to start life with an equal chance of happiness; this goal is not written in the stars and is no more an expression of what Kant called 'pure practical reason' than it is the Will of God; it is a goal worth dying for, but it does not require backup from supernatural forces." But I do not understand why taking into account the possibility of such a "backup from supernatural forces" must always be treated as a potential obstacle for moral progress. Sometimes, of course, faith in the existence of an absolute right and truth can be dangerous for social life, namely when someone tries to impose these values on other people. But sometimes it can also be the last hope of the oppressed.

It is often very difficult to say which kind of moral and political rhetoric will be most effective in a given historical and cultural situation. I think that only an analysis of a given context can decide this issue. A specific example of this dilemma is visible in Professor Rorty's well-known claim that we should renounce emancipatory rhetoric in favor of reformist rhetoric. I think that it would be more consistent with his own pragmatist attitude if he said that we should choose a given rhetoric according to a given context while taking account of possible profits and losses. The abandonment of emancipatory rhetoric is as much a dogmatic decision as is being true to it regardless of particular historical and political circumstances. It is true that reformist rhetoric is the most proper one for liberal Western democracies, but I am not sure that the same is true of still-existing totalitarian regimes.

As my last point, I should like to say that I accept most elements of Professor Rorty's critique of Professor Habermas's position. Nevertheless, I also think that from a pragmatist point of view one can see many valuable elements in Professor Habermas's thought connected, among other things, to its utopian dimension. I do not want to go into particulars of this theory. I wish to say only that regardless of different strengths and weaknesses, one thing seems to be very important. I am thinking of the particular critical aspects of Professor Habermas's theory which remind us of the distance yet to be traveled in our journey toward actual realizations of democratic principle. I think that we should take seriously Professor Habermas's critique of contemporary liberal states, expressed in many of his books. We should also listen to the other critical voices which have been raised in criticism of such states, portraying them as domains of manipulation rather than fulfilled democracy. In addition to Professor Habermas, I am thinking especially of Thomas McCarthy, Sheila Benhabib, and Richard Bernstein.

On the other hand, though, I completely agree with Professor Rorty that there is nothing more precious to preserve in social life than democracy and that we should avoid hysterical condemnation of its dark side. I think that at least sometimes, however, we need utopian thought to prevent ourselves from accepting the existing status quo. So I am inclined to treat Professor Habermas's theory, from the pragmatic point of view, as a very useful tool which one can employ when it is needed. I hope that Professor Rorty agrees with me, the more so since his own philosophy has a utopian dimension too.

For me it is clear that both Professor Habermas and Professor Rorty are members of the same family, so to speak. They want the same thing: a better, more democratic society, as just and as free as may be possible. They are both excellent social-democratic thinkers. The main difference between them consists of the rhetoric which they use to convince their audiences of the importance of social-democratic values and goals.

Maybe one could shed some final light on the difference between them by saying that Professor Habermas is a German thinker while Professor Rorty is an American one. In Germany, liberal democracy painfully failed at one time. In the United States, it never did. I think that only in the context of the different historical and cultural traditions of their countries can we fully understand their different positions. Anyway, from my particular point of view the most important thing is that they both think of democracy, freedom, and justice as most precious values, worthy of protection against any kind of activity which proclaims knowledge of a "better" arrangement of social life.

WLADYSLAW KRAJEWSKI

I am against pragmatism and the entirety of post-Nietzschean philosophy. I am a supporter of realist epistemology—of scientific realism, in particular—which has its origins in the works of Plato, Aristotle, Descartes, Locke, and many others. Contemporary scientific realism differs in many respects, though, from classical realism.

First, we now know that we never have whole and accurate truth. We now know that in our world knowledge is always partial and approximate, but we hope that in the course of the growth of science we may gain better and better approximations, an ever more complete picture of reality, and come closer and closer to the truth. Also, it is probable that this path is infinite. Maybe there are zigzags in it, and surely there are sometimes steps back; but the general direction is the direction toward the truth.

Second, I agree that we must take into account Darwinism, biology, and the causal connection between real processes and our brains—our minds—and that this was not taken into account earlier. But we must not consider causal connection a substitute for representation. On the contrary: Representation is impossible without causal connection; representation is always due to causal connection.

I agree that our theories are used in our struggle for a life, in coping with our environment: but this is because of their truth, their approximate truth. If we had false theories, we could not have any practical successes. Only approximately true theories can lead to successes.

Third, I agree that there is no sharp borderline between discovery and invention or between representation and intervention. We must intervene in nature (Ian Hacking wrote about this), but we intervene to have a better, deeper representation of reality. We combine discovery with invention and creation. We discover new, natural phenomena and their regularities. At the same time we create scientific concepts and theories. We do this not just for their own sake, however, but in order to have a better representation of reality. This is, of course, not a direct but rather an indirect and complicated representation. It is nevertheless, in the end, still a representation of reality.

Finally, the last problem has to do with the link with the sciences. I think that scientific realism connects better with the sciences than does pragmatism. What is the aim of science? Is it truth? Or practical usefulness? Of course it is both. But the first aim is truth, while the second aim is usefulness. Every scientific inquiry tends to the truth, to the description of reality, to the approximate description of reality. Many scientific inquiries also tend to practical usefulness and to application, but not all do. Maybe even those inquiries that do not now have practical usefulness as their objective may also have some application in the future; but scientific inquiries do not necessarily point to useful applications at the time of the investigation.

In the end, the question for Professor Rorty is this: Does he really believe that every scientist making an inquiry either does or should think about its practical use?

PIOTR GUTOWSKI

I have two points to make in regard to Professor Rorty's "Relativism: Finding and Making." The first one is of a historical nature and concerns the meaning of the terms "pragmatist tradition" or "American pragmatist tradition."

Rorty points to John Dewey, William James, Donald Davidson, and Hilary Putnam as the best representatives of that tradition. There is, however, one significant omission from this list, namely, Charles Sanders Peirce, who is usually recognized, at least in Poland, not only as the founder of pragmatism, but also as the most important of its exponents. Rorty mentioned him just once in his essay, in connection with the definition of belief.

This omission, together with the quite important differences between pragmatists (e.g., between Rorty and say Putnam or Nicholas Rescher) may suggest that we should talk about two pragmatist traditions or, maybe better, about two different streams within this movement: the universalist stream and the relativist stream. The first one would be connected with Peirce, and nowadays with the people like Rescher. The second stream is connected with Dewey and Rorty. Putnam would be somewhere in the middle. What Rorty describes as pragmatism would then be just one stream of this tradition.

To summarize my first concern: (1) I hope Professor Rorty will clarify the place of Peirce in his picture of the American pragmatist tradition, and (2) I wonder if he would agree with the above description of a pragmatist movement divided into two camps: (more) universalist and (more) relativist, or, as Rescher would put it, right wing and left wing.

My second point is an objection which could be entitled: "In Defense of Giraffes." It is directed against Rorty's main suggestion that the distinction between finding and making should be dropped because in fact we (as individuals, societies, or a genus) "make" everything, and nothing is "found" in the world. In other words, the claim appears to be that there is no objective world outside us. As the ancient sophists would put it: Man is the measure of all things.

It seems to me that if we dropped this distinction and followed Rorty's suggestion, the world we live in would make no sense. It is quite obvious that we make many things: We create various cultures, languages, science, and so on; but the rules of such creation are not wholly arbitrary. There are certain objective restrictions to this creativity, one of which is the fact that the world has some structure. It is quite evident not only in the physical sciences but also in our common sense perception.

Let me give a short example: As Professor Rorty ponders this objection of mine, I hope he will consider the big green giraffe, just behind him, that is trying to eat the violet leaves growing on his head. Is Professor Rorty able to see this giraffe? If not, can he make the giraffe be there, occupying part of what (probably) seems to be empty space? Rorty might say that he cannot do this as an individual, but that there might be some cultures where it is possible to do so. Or perhaps he will say that, ultimately, giraffes are only elements of our human world: There is no giraffe in the world of bats or frogs.

Well, I cannot imagine any culture creating the picture I sketched, for the simple reason that nobody can find green giraffes here in this portion of space and time and because there really are no leaves growing on Rorty's head. There has to be a certain composition of molecules in any portion of space we find that enables us to make anything, and this is also an objective restriction for any nonhuman "making." Obviously, someone might say that there is a giraffe here, but he or she would simply be wrong. Some of our creations are absurd because we make them without finding them first, such as certain awkward physical theories or the aforementioned big green giraffe behind Rorty.

ADAM CHMIELEWSKI

I happen to accept much of Professor Rorty's philosophy, but I would like to make two points and ask one question.

My first point is related to the obliteration of the distinction between philosophy, politics, and literature, which Rorty mentions as having been introduced by pragmatism. I do agree that these distinctions are dubious, and in my own philosophical practice I am often struck by the impossibility of distinguishing between these three allegedly distinct kinds of inquiry. I do agree that these names do not cut through any joints in the real world. However, I think that, perhaps paradoxically, there is a way of thinking in which these differences or limits can be reestablished. I think that they can also be given some kind of existence. Just because some people do think that the differences are there, they acquire some kind of reality to them. The point is that people do think that there are differences between these three kinds of inquiry or writing. These modes of inquiry are thus, so to speak, communally and socially reconstituted in this way.

My second point is concerned with the issue Professor Morawski mentioned earlier. I happen to agree with Rorty that intellectuals have no particular responsibility for the world and they are not custodians of meanings, obligations, morality, or anything like that. However, they are looked up to as custodians performing such a role by many people. For example, Rorty has himself mentioned his surprise that some news journals accuse him of being a proponent of some morally disastrous views, and that he is, so to speak, charged with responsibility. This is what I mean when I say that people look up to intellectuals—to philosophers—as people who are responsible for the world. Perhaps in this way we can, despite Rorty's disclaimers, attribute some responsibility to intellectuals, even if they acquire this responsibility just because they are thought to be responsible.

My question, finally, is related to questions formulated by other participants in this book. The question is, How did Professor Rorty come to adopt the view that he is adopting? Was he personally free to take Wittgenstein (late Wittgenstein, of course), Dewey, or Davidson, but not Peirce, for example, as his philosophical heroes? We heard one of the questioners declaring here, in a decisive way, that he rejects all these heroes and that he wishes to adopt different heroes. Why does Rorty adopt these particular thinkers as his spiritual ancestors? He might say that we come from different traditions and different communities and that we have different philosophical histories behind us. The question I am really asking here is, Is Rorty free to adopt any hero he wants? I ask him this because he very often talks as if he was an extreme voluntarist; that, despite his talk about communities, despite his talk about ethnicity, he seems to understand community as an aggregation of individuals, from among which one can choose freely those with whom one would like to associate. Is Rorty free—of his own free will—to belong to the community of philosophers with whom he associates himself? Or are there perhaps more important reasons than that for his doing so? Responding to one of the questions by Professor Habermas—that we can see ourselves as individuals or as parts of groups—Rorty used the phrase "my sense of myself as part of a group united by reciprocal loyalty [as opposed to] . . . my sense of myself as an isolated individual." I am making here a communitarian point: How far is it *his* sense and how far is his sense of being a part of a community or an individual—or anything—something that is itself created by some community? What community is Rorty coming from?

RICHARD RORTY

I will give very brief, dogmatic answers—we can argue about them later. Once again, I will start at the end and work backward.

My answer to the last question, what community do I come from, is the same as my answer to Professor Szahaj's earlier question. If you happen to come from an extraordinarily lucky, rich, and self-satisfied country—one which has enjoyed the rule of law uninterruptedly for two hundred years—you are likely to be more dismissive of legality and law and more interested in romance than if you come from a country where the rule of law has been in jeopardy. And I think that this is a predictable, psychological result. To leap back to Andrzej Szahaj's point, I think he is right that a pragmatist has to adapt his words to his audience. My emphasis on romance and prophecy and Whitman makes more sense against the background of the incredible luck that my country has happened to have. But I trust that you will take this into account. You know where I am coming from.

I do not think there is any answer to the question why I chose these three heroes—Dewey, Wittgenstein, and Heidegger—except they are the most radical figures I could find. They are the most romantic figures, the farthest out, the most prophetic. I have a taste, obviously, for far-out, radical romantics.

My answer to the question of whether one should not leave the science–literature–politics distinction alone, rather than trying to fuzz it up, is that I am not trying to suggest an immediate change in institutional structures. I am merely casting doubt on the philosophical rationale for thinking that those structures are more than useful contrivances. I think we should consider the possibility that the Greek way of thinking of inquiry and dividing up culture, and the Kantian way of doing both, are not the only alternatives. I want us to remember that there are other ways of dividing up culture which might be worth developing and exploring.

On the question of scientific realism, I think the realists' basic argument is that true beliefs produce practical success because they are true. That is a scientific explanation of the success of science. This seems to me a bad argument because to have a proper scientific explanation of the success of science you would have to have an independent test for truth, independent of your test for success. I do not think we have an independent test for the correspondence of a scientific theory to reality, independent of tests of its utility.

On the question about Peirce: I think of Peirce as a somewhat primitive kind of pragmatist. He is not nearly as radical or as interesting as James or Dewey. Peirce said that he had practically memorized the *Critique of Pure Reason* by the time he was twenty, and I can believe it. I think that was a disaster for Peirce. He became so thoroughly imbued with the Kantian outlook that he was never able to break with it.

I think his greatest contribution was suggesting that it would be better to talk about signs—or, if you like, language—than to talk about experience. I think the essays in which, as we say, he founded semiotics are as important for what Bergmann called the "linguistic turn" as the work of Frege. Ian Hacking has said that that "turn" was the joint product of Frege and Peirce, and that seems right. But I think that once you have acknowledged that contribution, there is not much more you can get out of Peirce. I think all the interest of pragmatism comes later, in James and Dewey.

Now about giraffes: I want to urge that if you have the distinction between the idiosyncratic and the intersubjective, or the relatively idiosyncratic and the relatively intersubjective, that is the only distinction you need to take care of real versus imaginary giraffes. You do not need a further distinction between the made and the found or the subjective and the objective. You do not need a distinction between reality and appearance, or between inside and outside, but only one between what you can get a reasonable consensus about and what you cannot.

I shall end by returning to Szahaj's question about what kind of rhetoric a pragmatist should use. I think that the kind of romantic prophecy that I am attributing to James and Dewey is only useful for people who have the leisure and freedom to indulge themselves in such romantic dreams. Pragmatism should not be taken as anything definite enough to give a good solid argument for. It should be taken as a suggestion of a possibility for the human future, as vague as the possibility that (to return to the example of Luther) was offered at the beginning of the Reformation. When Luther suggested that Christianity might be something very different than what Europe had known for centuries, this was a romantic prophecy. It turned out, oddly enough, to be accurate. It became self-fulfilling. Christianity did evolve into something radically different from medieval Catholicism. It need not have, but we look back and are glad that it did. (Or some of us, anyway, are glad that it did.) I would like to think that, given peace, luck, security, and money (though it is very improbable that we shall have all four of these), the world will look back at the romantic prophecy of the American pragmatists and say, "Hey, we're glad they thought of that, we're glad they suggested this particular romantic prospect." But the limits of prophecy and romance are, I take it, obvious. For most purposes, they are not very helpful. But sometimes, when historical conditions happen to be right, they can be very useful indeed.

Appendix III

Comments on Philosophy and the Dilemmas of the Contemporary World

DÉSIRÉE PARK

When Hume asserted that reason is and ought to be only the slave of the passions, one of the passions that he can plausibly be said to mean is the love of justice. This conforms with his claim that, while justice is a "nonnatural virtue," it is not an "arbitrary virtue." Good Scot that Hume was, he believed in the efficacy of education. It can thus be argued, with Hume, that the development of the love of justice can be founded on his principle of natural affections for one's family. A cultivated love of justice would then promote the recognition of the rights of the stranger, and thence of all human beings. My question, then, is this: Can the love of justice be inculcated, and would this not be a way of responding to xenophobia?

RAFAL WIERZCHOSLAWSKI

My question concerns what I would call the moral claims which follow from the theories of Professors Habermas and Rorty. I am especially concerned with the range of those claims—I mean their universal dimension. The question I would like to ask is whether this universal range should be somehow limited to certain kinds of societies only, *per analogiam* to the kind of self-limitation which has been invoked by John Rawls, from as early as his first claims in *The Theory of Justice*—that his theory is valid for any kind of society that focuses on such justice—to his latest works, where he limits his claims to well-ordered societies. This concept has a rather precise reference to social systems and political societies.

MAREK J. SIEMEK

I wonder if Professor Rorty could accept the possibility that for us, I mean not for *his* "us" but for us here in Central and Eastern Europe, the hierarchy of these values must be quite different. We accept, of course, Rorty's beautiful thesis about the priority of democracy to philosophy, but we were not "born modern," as it was beautifully put by Professor Gellner. We must instead grow up to modernity.

What we need here (I think we need this not only in Poland, but in all of Europe; especially, perhaps, in Central and Eastern Europe) is not so much this beautiful equality of all possible concepts and sources of inspiration, equating philosophy with science, philosophy with poetry, philosophy with politics. For us the most important thing is to find in philosophy—not *only* in philosophy but in philosophy too—a general framework for our mental and cultural rationalization and modernization. This is because what we lack is just this foundation, which for Rorty is obvious and self-evident; it is like window glass, which Rorty does not see because he sees through it. Our window glass is not as clean as his. We must, first of all, make our window glass clean because we still see it, and we see nothing through it. That is why what we need is not Nietzsche but Hegel—not romantic Hegel but rationalist Hegel; what we need is not Heidegger but Husserl; not Derrida, Lyotard, and Foucault, but John Rawls, Ernest Gellner, Leszek Kolakowski, Karl Otto Appel, and Jürgen Habermas. What we need are the conceptual and normative foundations of our social, mental, and cultural rationality, which Rorty takes for granted. It is because Rorty takes these foundations for granted that he can afford to speak, in such beautiful language, about the priority of democracy. We must still construct our democracy, and we cannot do it without philosophy, which must be in this sense prior to our democracy.

JÓZEF KOSIAN

To what extent were Lyotard and Derrida constructive inspirations for Rorty's philosophy? A second question, which was raised by my student, is this: How is Rorty's philosophy finally to be characterized? I proposed the following answer: Richard Rorty is a philosopher of the "American Dream."

By "American Dream," I understand first of all America's great contributions to the democratic heritage of the world, symbolized by the Bill of Rights and the Declaration of Independence. The Virginia Declaration, written by George Mason, guaranteed a free press, religious liberty and tolerance, trial by jury, and protection against unreasonable searches and seizures. This Virginia Declaration became the model for later constitutions and declarations of rights: for the French Declaration of the Rights of Man and of the Citizen (in which Lafayette played the leading role) and for the Belgian (1831) and Mexican (1857) Constitutions as well. The most inspiring of Rorty's ideas says that as long as dialogue goes on, there is hope for mutual understanding between all humankind.

I wonder if Rorty would agree with such a description.

MAREK BIELECKI

Regarding Professor Habermas's essay, I will quote two short sentences from a recent review by Martha Nussbaum of the book *A Mind of One's Own: Feminist Essays on Reason and Objectivity*. This review appeared in *The New York Review of Books*. Professor Nussbaum says that "Jürgen Habermas, on the Continent, is one of the thinkers who provide an account of how human interests might be sifted and critically examined in order to produce a process of knowledge-seeking that, while not free from interest, is free from illegitimate bias." Frankly speaking, I must confess that even after reading Habermas's paper, and based on my perhaps shallow understanding of his works, I still do not know how this could be achieved.

Professor Rorty says that he is very much concerned about the well-being of disadvantaged segments of the American population, such as racial minorities and women. Here is a quote from John Stuart Mill, taken from *The Subjugation of Women*. According-ing to Mill, "women's situation becomes far worse in eras mistrustful of reason and argument."

GRAZYNA SKAPSKA

I will return to the argument that Professor Habermas made about functionalism as a justification for the kind of Darwinian pragmatism that Professor Rorty is writing and talking about.

If functionalism justifies Darwinian pragmatism and if we assume that the main principle of functionalism is adaptivity—the ability to adapt oneself to a situation—and if, on the other hand, we have this principle of Darwinian pragmatism, which is the pursuit of one's own happiness, then, in that situation, how can we avoid a kind of political and moral opportunism? Surely such opportunism, which says that one must functionally adapt to a situation in pursuit of one's own happiness, is the inevitable result of those two principles working together.

To that main question are connected two subquestions. The first one involves the place of critical reason and the justification of critical reason (if any) in such a concept of a society, based as it is on Darwinian pragmatism. We know that democracy, anyway, cannot function without critical reason. So that is my question: Does Rorty provide, in his theory—and if so, where—any kind of justification of critical reason, which is deprived, on the one hand, of objective criteria for evaluating conditions and, on the other hand, of any subjective reason of the individual?

My second subquestion is connected to trust, which Professor Rorty mentioned in his answer to Professor Habermas. It is very difficult for me to connect trust with Darwinian pragmatism. But even if we could find a place for trust in Darwinian pragmatism, I would still have my own questions concerning civil society and democracy. Civil society, after all, functions with a certain distrust—or at least a limited trust—in democracy, in order to control it. What is the role of trust in Rorty's overall view?

JOHN T. SANDERS

I am not entirely sure about this, but I think I might just be one of Rorty's "us." My difficulty in being sure about this involves especially my lack of certainty concerning just what the boundaries of the relevant *ethnos* might be. But I hope to gain a bit of clarity from Rorty's answer to my question.

The case cited by Rorty, concerning the eventual adjustment of Europe to the Copernican worldview is a good place to begin, I think. Here is my problem: I understand pretty clearly why an *absolutist* might read Thomas Kuhn's detailed account of that transition as undermining the claim that progress toward the truth was made. In absolutist terms the story told by Kuhn does seem to me to subvert—and seems to Kuhn to subvert—the claims of progress and increasing verisimilitude. That is a large part of the reason why Karl Popper objected so strongly to Kuhn-style accounts of such periods in the history of science.

But pragmatists, as I understand them, have their own view of what truth and progress are. William James, quite famously, offered a straightforward pragmatic *definition* of truth, one which has persuaded many people not only within the United States, but all over the world. In rejecting in general the ideal of truth, I suspect that Rorty indicates thereby a rejection of this part of the pragmatic tradition. If so, I hope to learn why. But if not, perhaps Professor Rorty can clarify for me what stops a pragmatist—armed with the pragmatic definition of truth—from saying that progress toward the truth was made through the "Copernican revolution."

ANDRZEJ GRZEGORCZYK

Why did Professor Rorty not mention, as his ancestors, some very eminent pragmatists, namely Marx, Engels, Lenin, and Stalin? Marx said the same that he is saying, namely, that there is no problem concerning how things are, but rather that the problem is how to behave in order to change the world according to our desires. This is just what Rorty has said, and this principle was embodied in practice by both Lenin and Stalin.

My second question is also very sarcastic: Why does Rorty not apply his philosophy to himself? The application is very simple. If words are tools of our biological desires, as he says, then his way of philosophizing is a tool of his desire. Perhaps his desire is to dominate the intellectual market in philosophy, and this may be part of a more general target. Perhaps in order to understand Rorty's philosophy, we must take into consideration his personal goals, his professional business goals, and the common business goals of the entire U.S. economy. Professor Rorty is to be thanked for recalling for us the lesson of history we have been taught during the last fifty years.

RICHARD RORTY

If you concentrate on the Eleventh Thesis of Feuerbach, then it is easy to read Marx as a good pragmatist. Marx and Dewey have a great deal in common. They both wanted to naturalize Hegel. Marx was a historicist in Popper's bad sense of historicism, who thought he knew the deep meaning of human history. Dewey criticized him precisely for that—for having thought that he knew the very essence of history, and therefore being insufficiently experimental in his attitude toward social change. Dewey thought Marx was too confident in his proposal for the cure for social ills.

It might be worth mentioning here that Dewey was the principal intellectual spokesman for the anti-Communist left in the United States for some thirty years. He never in fact read much Marx, but I think he understood what had happened to Marxism quite well. So I think that it would be a mistake to think that if you are attracted to Thesis Eleven you are likely to leave the door open to Lenin and Stalin. You might just be leaving it open to Franklin Delano Roosevelt. Dewey's pragmatism was often treated as an intellectual apology for Roosevelt's "New Deal" (though Dewey himself had doubts about Roosevelt). That view of his pragmatism seems to me more plausible than seeing it as an apology for Stalinism.

I do not want to say that words are tools of biological desires. I think that we have broken free of biology by taking the evolution of our species into our own hands. We language-using animals are able not just to adapt to the environment, but to change both ourselves and our environment self-consciously and deliberately. This process cannot be described as satisfaction of a biological need without stripping the term "biological" of all clear meaning.

Like everyone else, I should be delighted to be able to dominate the intellectual market. But the role in the American economy of exporting philosophy professors is actually quite small. We missionaries of the "American Dream" do not really bring home much profit.

Let me now turn to the question Professor Sanders asked about whether progress toward the truth was made by Copernicus. Because of Copernicus, we can do many things that we could not do before, gratify many desires that we could not gratify before; we also became capable of richer, more interesting desires than we had before. But was progress *toward the truth* made? I have no idea. That is, for all I know or care, Copernicus will be completely outdated three centuries from now. For all I know or care, future maps of the heavens will make Copernicus look as bad as Copernicus made Aristotle look. Sufficient unto the millennium is the progress thereof. If we are moving closer to some final goal, that is nice. But I do not see how we would ever know whether we were closer to this final goal, and I do not see why we should care.

On the question about whether you can fit the notion of trust together with a Darwinian outlook: As I see it, the non–language-using animals tend to be antagonistic toward animals that are of the wrong species. They stick together in fairly tight groups. They do not form alliances between species. Because we have language, we cannot only domesticate (or, if you like, enslave) other species and other human communities, but we can form alliances with those communities: We can overcome tribal boundaries by creating, through the use of language, communities of trust.

One should not treat any commendation of Darwin as a symptom of reductionism and biologism. My references to Darwin are simply devices for directing your attention to the existence of a nondualist, non-Platonist, non-Kantian, naturalistic description of the human situation. They suggest a way of thinking of culture as continuous with biology by thinking of the development of language as an event in nature requiring no special magic, no foot in another world. We can then go on to think of the development of increasingly richer languages as, again, naturally explicable—no more difficult to understand than the development of increasingly more complicated flowers.

This does not mean, of course, that one could give a causal explanation in *biological* terms of the increased richness of human languages—an increase which is both cause and effect of the creation of larger and larger communities of trust. There is, as Husserl and everyone else keeps saying, no reduction of the intentional to the nonintentional. But there is nothing, I think, inherently reductive about pragmatism. Pragmatism tells you to use as many vocabularies as is useful to use and has no interest in reducing any of them to any of the others. Pragmatists think there is never any point in saying, "The *real* vocabulary for describing what's *really* going on is. . . ."

On the quotation from John Stuart Mill, according to which women's situations become even worse in eras which mistrust reason and argument, I think Mill should be interpreted as meaning "in religious eras." Mill and Harriett Taylor were very conscious of the patriarchal character of monotheistic Western religions. When he spoke of reason and argument, I do not think Mill had in mind a rationalist view, as opposed to a pragmatist view, of reason and argument. What he was commending was a culture in which anything can be put up for discussion, as opposed to a culture in which some things are immune from criticism.

The women's movement has depended much more on narrative example and image than on reason and argument. Consider a famous court case in Canada: The women of Canada noticed in 1927 that the Constitution of Canada says "any person may be elected to the Senate who . . ." without mentioning sex. So they said "Okay, so *we* can be elected to the Senate." The Supreme Court of Canada was asked whether "person" meant "man or woman" or "man." The argument of the feminist lawyers was that, in reading every other statute and constitutional provision, "person" had always been construed to mean "man or woman." The Supreme Court of Canada decided that that was true but that it would be so ridiculous to let a woman be a senator that in *this* case the word "person" just *had* to mean "man."

The feminist lawyers had an absolutely airtight argument, and it did not do them the slightest bit of good. Reason and argument were certainly valued in the Canadian judicial system, but the imagination of the judges was insufficient to let them change the practices of the society. I think it was a shift in imagination rather than an increased susceptibility to argument which eventually gave us female Canadian senators.

I guess I have already answered Professor Kosian's question: Am I a philosopher of the "American Dream?" I certainly am. Professor Gellner's description of my relation to America was exactly right. If you want a good narrative description of this American spirit, you should read Mark Twain's *A Connecticut Yankee in King Arthur's Court*. My attitude toward Kant and Weber is that of the Connecticut Yankee toward the culture of King Arthur's court (that is an overstatement, but you see what I mean).

In regard to the relation of institutional and cultural change in Central Europe to the Kantian framework of three autonomous cultural spheres, it seems to me quite true that in a country that has been ruled by, so to speak, a false romanticism—the romanticism of Marxism–Leninism—and in which the basic structures of constitutional democracies are still being put back in place, this American romance is, for the time being, not of much use. My romanticized version of the American Dream may not be what Poland really needs to hear about at the moment.

A friend of mine in Prague said that the trouble with the Czech Republic under its present Prime Minister is that they are trying to have the administration of Ronald Reagan without ever having had the "New Deal" administration of Franklin Roosevelt. That is, they are trying to have the contemporary free-market American ideology without ever having instituted the welfare state. It seems to me that there is not much use for my brand of futuristic romanticism until you have established the standard institutions of constitutional democracy—institutions which do, to be sure, presuppose the autonomy of these three cultural spheres.

To return to the topic of American luck: In a rich, secure, lucky country, which has had these institutions in place for a long time, there may be room for experimentation and romance. Perhaps if America had succeeded in constructing a full-fledged welfare state (of the sort which the Dutch and the Danes presently enjoy) there would be less support for the conservative reaction we are presently seeing in American politics. But Roosevelt and his democratic successors did not do enough to provide the poor in America with a safety net, so the present reactionary trend of American politics is a potential disaster.

Let me now turn to the question that was raised about the priority of democracy to philosophy and about Rawls's later writings. In those writings, Rawls limits the applicability of the theory of justice of political liberalism to what he calls "reasonable people." That is, people who hold reasonable comprehensive views. I think that he is right, but the question this view raises is the one at issue in the exchange between Rawls and Jürgen Habermas in a recent issue of *The Journal of Philosophy*. That question is: Do you want or need universalistic arguments for the desirability of being what Rawls calls reasonable, or should you simply take the reasonableness of a certain group, population, nation, and so on as a desideratum which cannot be argued for?

I understand Rawls to be opting for the latter alternative and saying that when formulating the law of peoples, you are formulating a law for peoples who are reasonable enough to join us in a cooperative community. Some people are not that reasonable. We have no argument about why they should be more reasonable. We can only say "Sorry, we cannot work with you." Habermas thinks that there is more to be done here. He thinks, so to speak, that philosophers can do more work than Rawls thinks them able to do. Here I am on Rawls's side of the argument.

ERNEST GELLNER

I share Professor Rorty's appreciation (perhaps he feels more strongly about it) of the "American Dream." It seems to me nothing could be better for humankind than if it came to resemble a small New England town, with its security, prosperity, tolerance, and individualism. The disagreement is about what one says about it. The trouble with pragmatism is that it sees it as a fruit of continuity, which, in fact, in America it was. Anywhere else in the world it is the fruit of discontinuity. The issue is between continuity, which is what pragmatism says is the secret of life, and discontinuity, which is, it seems to me, the reality. That is the basic and practical important disagreement, which will have to be thought about more.

»» ««

Bibliography

Edited by Stanislaw Butryn. Works are arranged chronologically.

SELECTED BIBLIOGRAPHY OF JÜRGEN HABERMAS

Books

Das Absolute und die Geschichte. Von der Zwiespältigkeit in Schellings Denken. Dissertationsdruck. Bonn: Bouvier, 1954.

Student und Politik. Eine soziologische Untersuchung zum politischen Bewußtsein Frankfurter Studenten. Coauthors: Ludwig von Friedeburg, Christoph Oehler, and Friedrich Weltz. Neuwied/Berlin: Luchterhand, 1961.

Strukturwandel der Öfftentlichkeit. Untersuchungen zu einer Kategorie der bürgerlichen Gesellschaft. Neuwied/Berlin: Luchterhand, 1962. With a new foreword, Frankfurt am Main: Suhrkamp, 1990.

Theorie und Praxis. Sozialphilosophische Studien. Neuwied/Berlin: Luchterhand, 1963. New edition, Frankfurt am Main: Suhrkamp, 1971.

Erkenntnis und Interesse. Frankfurt am Main: Suhrkamp, 1968. New edition, 1973.

Technik und Wissenschaft als Ideologie. Frankfurt am Main: Suhrkamp, 1968.

Protestbewegung und Hochschulreform. Frankfurt am Main: Suhrkamp, 1969.

Zur Logik der Sozialwissenschaften. Frankfurt am Main: Suhrkamp, 1970. Enlarged edition, 1981.

Philosophisch-politische Profile. Frankfurt am Main: Suhrkamp, 1971. Enlarged edition, 1981.

Theorie der Gesellschaft oder Sozialtechnologie. Coauthor: Niklas Luhmann. Frankfurt am Main: Suhrkamp, 1971.
Legitimationsprobleme im Spätkapitalismus. Frankfurt am Main: Suhrkamp, 1973.
Zur Rekonstruktion des Historischen Materialismus. Frankfurt am Main: Suhrkamp, 1976.
Politik, Kunst, Religion. Stuttgart: Reclam, 1978.
Kleine Politische Schriften I-IV. Frankfurt am Main: Suhrkamp, 1981.
Theorie des kommunikativen Handelns. Frankfurt am Main: Suhrkamp, 1981.
Moralbewußtsein und kommunikatives Handeln. Frankfurt am Main: Suhrkamp, 1983.
Vorstudien und Ergänzungen zur Theorie des kommunikativen Handelns. Frankfurt am Main: Suhrkamp, 1984.
Der philosophische Diskurs der Moderne. Frankfurt am Main: Suhrkamp, 1985.
Die Neue Unübersichtlichkeit. Frankfurt am Main: Suhrkamp, 1985.
Eine Art Schadensabwicklung. Frankfurt am Main: Suhrkamp, 1987.
Nachmetaphysisches Denken. Frankfurt am Main: Suhrkamp, 1988.
Die nachholende Revolution. Frankfurt am Main: Suhrkamp, 1990.
Erläuterungen zur Diskursethik. Frankfurt am Main: Suhrkamp, 1991.
Texte und Kontexte. Frankfurt am Main: Suhrkamp, 1991.
Faktizität und Geltung. Frankfurt am Main: Suhrkamp, 1992.
Vergangenheit als Zukunft. München: Piper, 1993.
Die Normalität einer Berliner Republik. Frankfurt am Main: Suhrkamp, 1995.

Articles

Knowledge and Interest. *Inquiry* 9 (Winter 1966): 285–300.
On Systematically Distorted Communication. *Inquiry* 13 (Fall 1970): 205–218.
Towards a Theory of Communicative Competence. *Inquiry* 13 (Winter 1970): 360–375.
On Social Identity. *Telos* 19 (Spring 1974): 91–103.
Psychic Thermidor and the Rebirth of Rebellious Subjectivity. *Praxis* 1 (April 1981): 79–86.
A Reply to My Critics. In *Habermas: Critical Debates*, ed. D. Held, 219–283. Cambridge: MIT Press, 1982.
Reply to Skjei's "A Comment on Performative, Subject, and Proposition in Habermas's Theory of Communication." *Inquiry* 28 (March 1985): 105–112.
The New Obscurity: The Crisis of the Welfare State and the Exhaustion of Utopian Energies. *Philosophy and Social Criticism* 11 (Winter 1986): 1–18.

Towards a Communication-Concept of Rational Collective Will-Formation: A Thought-Experiment. *Ratio Juris* 2 (July 1989): 144–154.

Work and "Weltanschauung": The Heidegger Controversy from a German Perspective. *Critical Inquiry* 15 (Winter 1989): 431–456.

Comments on Searle: "Meaning, Communication, and Representation." In *John Searle and His Critics*, ed. E. LePore. Oxford: Blackwell, 1991.

Citizenship and National Identity: Some Reflections on the Future of Europe. *Praxis International* 12 (April 1992): 1–19.

A Generation Apart from Adorno. An Interview. *Philosophy and Social Criticism* 18 (1992): 119–124.

Work and "Weltanschauung." In *Heidegger: A Critical Reader*, ed. H. L. Dreyfus. Cambridge, Mass.: Blackwell, 1992.

Morality and Ethical Life: Does Hegel's Critique of Kant Apply to Discourse Ethics? In *Kant and Political Philosophy*, ed. R. Beiner. New Haven: Yale University Press, 1993.

Remarks on the Development of Horkheimer's Work. In *On Max Horkheimer*, ed. S. Benhabib. Cambridge: MIT Press, 1993.

Struggles for Recognition in Constitutional States. *European Journal of Philosophy* 1 (August 1993): 128–155.

The Critique of Reason as an Unmaking of the Human Sciences: Michel Foucault. In *Critique and Power*, ed. M. Kelly. Cambridge: MIT Press, 1994.

Postscript to "Faktizitat und Geltung." *Philosophy and Social Criticism* 20 (1994): 135–150.

Some Questions Concerning the Theory of Power: Foucault Again. In *Critique and Power*, ed. M. Kelly. Cambridge: MIT Press, 1994.

Taking Aim at the Heart of the Present: On Foucault's Lecture on Kant's "What is Enlightenment?" In *Critique and Power*, ed. M. Kelly. Cambridge: MIT Press, 1994.

Human Rights and Popular Sovereignty: The Liberal and Republican Versions. *Ratio Juris* 7 (March 1994): 1–13.

Three Normative Models of Democracy. *Constellation* 1 (April 1994): 1–10.

Reconciliation through the Public Use of Reason: Remarks on John Rawls' Political Liberalism. *Journal of Philosophy* 92 (March 1995): 109–131.

On the Internal Relation between the Rule of Law and Democracy. *European Journal of Philosophy* 3 (April 1995): 12–20.

Peirce and Communication. In *Peirce and Contemporary Thought: Philosophical Inquiries*, ed. K. L. Ketner. New York: Fordham University Press, 1995.

For detailed bibliography see the following:

Görtzen, René. *Jürgen Habermas: Eine Bibliographie seiner Schriften und der Secundärliteratur 1952–1981*. Frankfurt am Main: Suhrkamp, 1982.

Görtzen, René. Jürgen Habermas: A Bibliography. In *Reading Habermas*, ed. D. M. Rasmussen, 114–140. Oxford: Basil Blackwell, 1990.

Oraa, Jose Maria Aquirre. Jürgen Habermas: Bibliografia de 1981–1990. *Scriptorum Victoriense* 39 (1992): 126–172.

Douramanis, Demetrios. *Mapping Habermas, From German to English 1952–1995, a Bibliography of Primary Literature*. Sidney: ed. Eurotext, 1995.

SELECTED BIBLIOGRAPHY OF LESZEK KOLAKOWSKI

Books

Filozofski eseji. Beograd: Nolit, 1964.

Der Himmelsschlüssel. Erbauliche Geschichten. München: Piper, 1964.

Traktat über die Sterblichkeit der Vernunft. München: Piper, 1967.

Gespräche mit dem Teufel. Acht Diskurse über das Böse und zwei Stücke. München: Piper, 1968.

Chrétiens sans Église. La conscience religieuse el le lieu confessionel au XVII e siécle. Paris: Gallimard, 1969.

Geist und Ungeist christlicher Traditionen. Stuttgart: Kohlhammer, 1971.

Die Philosophie des Positivismus. München: Piper, 1971.

Der revolutionäre Geist. Stuttgart: Kohlhammer, 1972.

The Devil and Scripture. London: Oxford University Press, 1973.

Die Gegenwärtigkeit des Mythos. München: Piper, 1973.

The Socialist Idea: A Reappraisal. Eds. L. Kolakowski and S. Hampshire. London: Weidenfeld & Nicholson, 1974.

Husserl and the Search for Certitude. New Haven: Yale University Press, 1975.

Der Mensch ohne Alternative. Von der Möglichkeit und Unmöglichkeit Marxist zu sein. München: Piper, 1976.

Leben trotz Geschichte. München: Piper, 1977.

L'esprit révolutionnaire. Suivi de Marxisme: utopie et antiutopie. Bruxelles: Complexe, 1978.

Main Current of Marxism. Its Rise, Growth and Dissolution. 3 vols. Oxford: Clarendon Press, 1978.

Religion: If There Is No God. New York: Oxford University Press, 1982.

Bergson. New York: Oxford University Press, 1985.

L'esprit révolutionnaire. Paris: Denoël, 1985.

Philosophie de la religion. Paris: Fayard, 1985.

Le village introuvable. Paris: Complexe, 1986.

Metaphysical Horror. Oxford: Blackwell, 1988.

Modernity on Endless Trial. Chicago: University of Chicago Press, 1990.

God Owes Us Nothing: A Brief Remark on Pascal's Religion and on the Spirit of Jansenism. Chicago: University of Chicago Press, 1995.

Articles

The Persistence of the Sein-Sollen Dilemma. *Man World* 10 (1977): 194–233.

Beyond Empiricism: The Need for a Metaphysical Foundation for Freedom. In *On Freedom*, ed. J. Howard, 27–38. Greenwich: Devin-Adair, 1984.

Irrationality in Politics. *Dialectica* 39 (1985): 279–290.

Even When the Devil Says He Is Telling the Truth, He Is Lying. *Dialog and Humanism* 2 (1992): 11–17.

On the Practicability of Liberalism: What About the Children? *Critical Review* 7 (Winter 1993): 1–13.

Ethics. *Dialog and Humanism* 4 (1994): 5–44.

BIBLIOGRAPHY OF RICHARD RORTY

Books

The Linguistic Turn. Ed. R. Rorty. Chicago: University of Chicago Press, 1967; second, enlarged edition, 1992.

Exegesis and Argument: Essays in Greek Philosophy Presented to Gregory Vlastos. Eds. R. Rorty, E. Lee, and A. Mourelatos. Amsterdam: Van Gorcum, 1973.

Philosophy and the Mirror of Nature. Princeton: Princeton University Press, 1979. Translations: Chinese, German, Italian, Spanish, Portuguese, French, Serbo-Croatian, Japanese, Polish, Greek, Bulgarian, and Russian.

Consequences of Pragmatism. Minneapolis: University of Minnesota Press, 1982. Translations: Italian, Japanese, Serbo-Croatian, French, and Spanish.

Philosophy in History. Eds. R. Rorty, J. B. Schneewind, and Q. Skinner. Cambridge: Cambridge University Press, 1985. Partial translation: Spanish.

Contingency, Irony, and Solidarity. Cambridge: Cambridge University Press, 1988. Translations: German, Italian, Spanish, Dutch, Danish, French, Hungarian, Polish, Greek, Turkish, Chinese, Serbo-Croatian, Czech, and Russian.

Objectivity, Relativism and Truth: Philosophical Papers I. Cambridge: Cambridge University Press, 1991. Essays included in this volume are indicated in the Articles and Reviews section with "ORT." Translations: Italian, French, and Hungarian.

Essays on Heidegger and Others: Philosophical Papers II. Cambridge: Cambridge University Press, 1991. Essays included in this volume are indicated in the Articles and Reviews section with "EHO." Translations: Italian, Spanish, French, and Hungarian.

Hoffnung statt Erkenntnis: Einleitung in die Pragmatische Philosophie. Vienna: Passagen Verlag, 1994. The French version appeared as *L'Espoir au lieu de savoir: introduction au pragmatisme.* Paris: Albin Michel, 1995. Russian and Hungarian translations are in preparation.

Collections of Articles in Foreign Translation

Solidarität oder Objectivität? Ditzingen: Reclam Verlag, 1988. Contains Solidarity or Objectivity; The Priority of Democracy to Philosophy, and Freud and Moral Reflection.

Philosophy of/for Solidarity and Freedom: Beyond the Illusions of Dualisms. Eds. R. J. Tetsugaku and N. G. Koete. Tokyo: Iwanami Shoten, 1988. Contains Science as Solidarity; Texts and Lumps; Pragmatism without Method; The Historiography of Philosophy: Four Genres; The Priority of Democracy to Philosophy; and Pragmatism, Davidson and Truth.

Solidariteit of Objectiviteit: Drie filosofische essays. Meppel: Uitgeverij Boom, 1990. Dutch translation of the three essays included in *Solidarität oder Objectivität?*

Verite sans Pouvoir: la Philosophie sans Authorite. Paris: Editions de l'Eclat, 1990. Contains Pragmatism, Davidson and Truth; Science as Solidarity; Is Natural Science a Natural Kind?; and Deconstruction and Circumvention.

Hou Zhe Xue Wen Hua [Towards a Post-Philosophical Culture]. Shanghai: Shang Hai Yi Wen Chu Ban She, 1991. Contains Chinese translations of Introduction to Consequences of Pragmatism; Philosophy as Science, as Metaphor, and as Politics; Is Natural Science a Natural Kind?; Deconstruction; Anti-Essentialism and the Literary Left; The Priority of Democracy to Philosophy; Postmodernist Bourgeois Liberalism; Pragmatism, Davidson and Truth; Pragmatism, Relativism and Irrationalism; and Science as Solidarity.

Heidegger, Wittgenstein en Pragmatisme. Amsterdam: Uitgeverij Kok Agora, 1992. Contains Pragmatism without Method; Texts and Lumps; Inquiry as Recontextualization; Philosophy as Science, as Metaphor, and as Politics; Heidegger, Contingency and Pragmatism; and Wittgenstein, Heidegger and the Reification of Language.

Eine Kultur ohne Zentrum: Vier phiosophische Essays. Stuttgart: Reclam, 1993. Contains Is Natural Science a Natural Kind?; Non-Reductive Physicalism; Heidegger, Kundera and Dickens; and Deconstruction and Circumvention.

Chung Wei Literary Monthly 22, no. 7 (December 1993). A Rorty issue containing Chinese translations of Trotsky and the Wild Orchids; A Pragmatist View of Rationality and Cultural Difference; Feminism and Pragmatism; Deconstruction; and Comments on Eco.

La Svolta Linguistica. Milan: Garzanti, 1994. Contains Italian translations of Metaphysical Difficulties of Linguistic Philosophy; Why Does Language Matter to Philosophy?—Ten Years Later; and Twenty-Five Years Later.

Articles and Reviews

Initials of book titles indicate that the piece was reprinted in *Consequences of Pragmatism* (CP), *Objectivity, Relativism and Truth* (ORT), or *Essays on Heidegger and Others* (EHO).

Review of Experience and the Analytic: A Reconsideration of Empiricism, by Alan Pasch. *International Journal of Ethics* 70 (October 1959): 75–77.

Review of Modern Science and Human Freedom, by David L. Miller. *International Journal of Ethics* 70 (April 1960): 248–249.

Review of John Dewey: His Thought and Influence. Ed. J. Blewett. *Teacher's College Record* 62 (October 1960): 88–89.

Pragmatism, Categories and Language. *Philosophical Review* 70 (April 1961): 197–223.

Recent Metaphilosophy. *Review of Metaphysics* 15 (December 1961): 299–318.

The Limits of Reductionism. In *Experience, Existence and the Good*, ed. I. C. Lieb, 100–116. Carbondale: Southern Illinois University Press, 1961.

Review of Introduction to the Philosophy of History, by Raymond Aron. *The New Leader* 25 (December 1961): 18–19.

Review of American Pragmatism: Peirce, James and Dewey, by Edward C. Moore. *International Journal of Ethics* 72 (January 1962): 146–147.

Second Thoughts on Teaching Communism. *Teacher's College Record* 63 (April 1962).

Realism, Categories, and the "Linguistic Turn." *International Philosophical Quarterly* 2 (May 1962): 307–322.

Review of The Value Judgment, by W. D. Lamont. *Journal for the Scientific Study of Religion* 2 (Fall 1962): 139–140.

Empiricism, Extensionalism and Reductionism. *Mind* 72 (April 1963): 176–186.

Review of Understanding Whitehead, by Victor Lowe. *Journal of Philosophy* 60 (25 April 1963): 246–251.

Review of Utopian Essays and Practical Proposals, by Paul Goodman. *Teacher's College Record* 64 (May 1963): 743–744.

The Subjectivist Principle and the Linguistic Turn. In *Alfred North Whitehead: Essays on His Philosophy*, ed. G. L. Kline, 134–157. New Jersey: Prentice-Hall, 1963.

Matter and Event. In *The Concept of Matter*, ed. E. McMullin, 497–524. Notre Dame, Ind.: Notre Dame University Press, 1963. A revised version appears in *Explorations in Whitehead's Philosophy*, eds. L. Ford and G. Kline, 68–103. New York: Fordham University Press, 1983.

Review of Reason and Analysis, by Brand Blanshard. *Journal of Philosophy* 60 (12 September 1963): 551–557.

Comments on Prof. Hartshorne's Paper. *Journal of Philosophy* 60 (10 October 1963): 606–608.

Review of Chauncy Wright and the Foundations of Pragmatism, by Edward H. Madden. *Philosophical Review* 73 (April 1964): 287–289.

Questions to Weiss and Tillich. In *Philosophical Interrogations*, eds. B. Rome and S. Rome, 266–267, 369–370, 392–393. New York: Holt, Rinehart and Winston, 1964.

Review of Clarity Is Not Enough: Essays in Criticism of Linguistic Philosophy, by H. D. Lewis. *International Philosophical Quarterly* 4 (1964): 623–624.

Mind-Body Identity, Privacy, and Categories. *Review of Metaphysics* 19 (September 1965): 24–54. Also in *Philosophy of Mind*, ed. S. Hampshire, 30–62. New York: Harper & Row, 1966; *Materialism and the Mind-Body Problem*, ed. D. M. Rosenthal, 174–199. New Jersey: Prentice-Hall, 1971; *Modern Materialism: Readings on Mind-Body Identity*, ed. J. O'Connor, 145–174. New York: Harcourt, Brace & World, 1969.

Aristotle. In *The American Peoples' Encyclopedia*. Vol. 2, ed. W. D. Scott, 399–400. Spencer Press, 1966.

Review of Charles Peirce and Scholastic Realism: A Study of Peirce's Relation to John Duns Scotus, by John F. Boler. *Philosophical Review* 75 (January 1966): 116–119.

Introduction. In *The Linguistic Turn*, ed. R. Rorty, 1–39. Chicago: University of Chicago Press, 1967.

Intuition. In *The Encyclopedia of Philosophy*. Vol. 4, ed. P. Edwards, 204–212. New York: Macmillan and Free Press, 1967.

Relations, Internal and External. In *The Encyclopedia of Philosophy*. Vol 7, ed. P. Edwards, 125–133. Macmillan and Free Press, 1967.

Review of Metaphysics, Reference and Language, by James W. Cornman. *Journal of Philosophy* 64 (23 November 1967): 770–774.

Do Analysts and Metaphysicians Disagree? *Proceedings of The Catholic Philosophical Association* 41 (1967): 39–53.

Review of Science and Metaphysics: Variations on Kantian Themes, by Wilfrid Sellars. *Philosophy* 45 (March 1970): 66–70.

Incorrigibility as the Mark of the Mental. *Journal of Philosophy* 67 (25 June 1970): 399–429.

Wittgenstein, Privileged Access, and Incommunicability. *American Philosophical Quarterly* 7 (July 1970): 192–205.

In Defense of Eliminative Materialism. *Review of Metaphysics* 24 (September 1970): 112–121. Also in *Materialism and the Mind-Body Problem*, ed. D. M. Rosenthal, 223–231. New Jersey: Prentice-Hall, 1971.

Strawson's Objectivity Argument. *Review of Metaphysics* 24 (December 1970): 207–244.

Cartesian Epistemology and Changes in Ontology. In *Contemporary American Philosophy*, ed. J. E. Smith, 273–292. New York: Humanities Press, 1970.

Review of The Origins of Pragmatism: Studies in the Philosophy of Charles Sanders Peirce and William James, by A. J. Ayer. *Philosophical Review* 80 (January 1971): 96–100.

Verificationism and Transcendental Arguments. *Nous* 5 (Fall 1971): 3–14.

Indeterminacy of Translation and of Truth. *Synthese* 23 (March 1972): 443–462.

Functionalism, Machines, and Incorrigibility. *Journal of Philosophy* 69 (20 April 1972): 203–220.

Dennett on Awareness. *Philosophical Studies* 23 (April 1972): 153–162.

The World Well Lost. *Journal of Philosophy* 69 (26 October 1972): 649–665. CP.

Review of Nihilism, by Stanley Rosen. *The Philosophy Forum* 11 (1972): 102–108.

Criteria and Necessity. *Nous* 7 (November 1973): 313–329.

Genus as Matter: A Reading of Metaphysics Z-H. In *Exegesis and Argument: Essays in Greek Philosophy Presented to Gregory Vlastos*, eds. R. Rorty, E. N. Lee, and A. P. O. Mourelatos, 393–420. Assen: Van Gorcum, 1973.

More on Incorrigibility. *Canadian Journal of Philosophy* 4 (September 1974): 195–197.

Matter as Goo: Comments on Grene's Paper. *Synthese* 25 (September 1974): 71–77.

Keeping Philosophy Pure. *The Yale Review* 65 (Spring 1976): 336–356. CP.

Realism and Reference. *The Monist* 59 (July 1976): 321–340.

Realism and Necessity: Milton Fisk's "Nature and Necessity." *Nous* 10 (September 1976): 345–354.

Review of On Human Conduct, by Michael Oakeshott, and Knowledge and Politics, by Roberto Mangabiera Unger. *Social Theory and Practice* 4 (Fall 1976): 107–116.

Overcoming the Tradition: Heidegger and Dewey. *Review of Metaphysics* 30 (December 1976): 280–305. CP.

Professionalized Philosophy and Transcendalist Culture. *The Georgia Review* 30 (1976): 757–769. CP.

Wittgensteinian Philosophy and Empirical Psychology. *Philosophical Studies* 31 (March 1977): 151–172.

Dewey's Metaphysics. In *New Studies in the Philosophy of John Dewey*, ed. S. Cahn, 45–74. Hanover: University of New England Press, 1977. CP.

Review of Why Does Language Matter to Philosophy? by Ian Hacking. *Journal of Philosophy* 74 (July 1977): 416–432.

Derrida on Language, Being and Abnormal Philosophy. *Journal of Philosophy* 74 (November 1977): 673–681.

Epistemological Behaviorism and the De-Transcendentalization of Analytic Philosophy. *Neue Hefte für Philosophie* 14 (1978): 117–142. Also in *Hermeneutics and Praxis*, ed. R. Hollinger, 89–121. Notre Dame, Ind.: University of Notre Dame Press, 1985.

A Middle Ground between Neurons and Holograms? *The Behavioural and Brain Sciences* 2 (1978): 248.

Philosophy as a Kind of Writing: An Essay on Derrida. *New Literary History* 10 (Autumn 1978): 141–160. CP.

From Epistemology to Hermeneutics. *Acta Philosophica Fennica* 30 (1978): 11–30.

Transcendental Argument, Self-Reference, and Pragmatism. In *Transcendental Arguments and Science*, eds. P. Bieri, R.-P. Horstman, and L. Krueger, 77–103. Dordrecht: D. Reidel, 1979.

The Unnaturalness of Epistemology. In *Body, Mind and Method: Essays in Honor of Virgil C. Aldrich*, eds. D. Gustafson and B. Tapscott, 77–92. Dordrecht: D. Reidel, 1979.

Pragmatism, Relativism and Irrationalism. *Proceedings and Addresses of the American Philosophical Association* 53 (August 1980): 719–738. CP.

Idealism, Holism, and the "Paradox of Knowledge." In *The Philosophy of Brand Blanshard*, ed. P. A. Schilpp, 719–738. La Salle, Ill.: Open Court, 1980.

Kripke vs. Kant. Review of Naming and Necessity, by Saul Kripke. *London Review of Books* (4 September 1980): 4–5.

On Worldmaking. Review of Ways of Worldmaking, by Nelson Goodman. *The Yale Review* 69 (1980): 276–279.

Reply to Dreyfus and Taylor. *Review of Metaphysics* 34 (September 1980): 39–46.

A Discussion. Coauthors: Hubert Dreyfus and Charles Taylor. *Review of Metaphysics* 34 (September 1980): 47–55.

Searle and the Secret Powers of the Brain. *The Behavioral and Brain Sciences* 3 (1980): 445–446.

Freud, Morality, and Hermeneutics. *New Literary History* 12 (Autumn 1980): 177–185.

Is There a Problem about Fictional Discourse? *Funktionen Des Fictiven: Poetic und Hermeneutik* 10. Munich: Fink Verlag, 1981. CP.

Review of American Sociology and Pragmatism, by J. D. Lewis and R. L. Smith. *Review of Metaphysics* 35 (1981): 147.

Reply to Professor Yolton. *Philosophical Books* 22 (1981): 134–135.

Nineteenth-Century Idealism and Twentieth-Century Textualism. *The Monist* 64 (1981): 155–174. CP.

From Epistemology to Romance: Cavell on Skepticism. *Review of Metaphysics* 34 (1981): 759–774. CP.

Beyond Nietzsche and Marx. Review of three books by or about Foucault. *London Review of Books* (19 February 1981): 5–6.

Method, Social Science, and Social Hope. *The Canadian Journal of Philosophy* 11 (1981): 569–588. CP.

Being Business. Review of A Heidegger Critique, by Roger Waterhouse. *Times Literary Supplement* (3 July 1981): 760.

Review of The Calling of Sociology and Other Essays, by Edward Shils. *Review of Metaphysics* 35 (1981): 167–168.

Philosophy in America Today. *The American Scholar* 51 (1982): 183–200. CP.

Persuasive Philosophy. Review of Philosophical Explanations, by Robert Nozick. *London Review of Books* (20 May 1982): 10–11.

From Philosophy to Post-Philosophy. Interview. *Radical Philosophy* (Autumn 1982): 10–11.

Introduction. In *Consequences of Pragmatism*, xiii–xlvii. Minneapolis: University of Minnesota Press, 1982. Reprinted as Pragmatism and Philosophy. In *After Philosophy*, eds. K. Bayles, J. Bohman, and T. McCarthy, 26–66. 1987. Abridged version appeared as The Fate of Philosophy. *The New Republic* (18 October 1982): 28–34.

Contemporary Philosophy of Mind. *Synthese* 53 (November 1982): 323–348.

Comments on Dennett. *Synthese* 53 (November 1982): 181–187.

Brute and Raw Experience. Review of Philosophy in the Twentieth Century, by A. J. Ayer. *The New Republic* (6 December 1982): 33–36.

Hermeneutics, General Studies, and Teaching. *Synergos* 2 (1982): 1–15.

The Pragmatist. Review of A Stroll with William James, by Jacques Barzun. *The New Republic* (9 May 1983): 32–34.

Unsoundness in Perspective. Review of Nietzsche, by R. Schacht, and Nietzsche and Philosophy, by G. Deleuze. *Times Literary Supplement* (17 June 1983): 619–620.

Against Belatedness. Review of The Legitimacy of the Modern Age, by Hans Blumenberg. *The London Review of Books* (16 June 1983): 3–5.

What Are Philosophers For? *The Center Magazine* (September/October 1983): 40–44.

Pragmatism Without Method. In *Sidney Hook: Philosopher of Democracy and Humanism*, ed. P. Kurtz, 259–273. Buffalo: Prometheus Books, 1983. ORT.

Postmodernist Bourgeois Liberalism. *The Journal of Philosophy* 80 (October 1983): 583–589. ORT.

Habermas and Lyotard on Post-Modernity. *Praxis International* 4 (April 1984): 32–44. Also in *Habermas and Post-Modernity*, ed. R. J. Bernstein, 161–176. Cambridge: Polity Press, 1985. EHO.

A Reply To Six Critics. *Analyse & Kritik* 6 (June 1984): 78–98.

Heidegger Wider den Pragmatisten. *Neue Hefte für Philosophie* 23 (1984): 1–22. EHO.

Deconstruction and Circumvention. *Critical Inquiry* 11 (September 1984): 1–23. EHO.

Solidarity or Objectivity. *Nanzan Review of American Studies* 6 (1984): 1–19. Also in *Post-Analytic Philosophy*, eds. J. Rajchman and C. West, 3–19. New York: Columbia University Press, 1985. Presented as *Relativism*, the Howison Lecture at University of California at Berkeley, 31 January 1983. ORT.

Signposts Along the Way That Reason Went. Review of Margins of Philosophy, by Jacques Derrida. *London Review of Books* (16 February 1984): 5–6.

Introduction. Coauthors: J. B. Schneewind and Q. Skinner. In *Philosophy in History*, eds. R. Rorty, J. B. Schneewind, and Q. Skinner, 1–14. Cambridge: Cambridge University Press, 1984.

The Historiography of Philosophy: Four Genres. In *Philosophy in History*, ed. R. Rorty, J. B. Schneewind, and Q. Skinner, 49–75. Cambridge: Cambridge University Press, 1984.

What's It All About? Review of Intentionality, by John Searle. *London Review of Books* (17 May 1984): 3–4.

Life at the End of Inquiry. Review of *Realism and Reason: Philosophical Papers III*, by Hilary Putnam. *London Review of Books* (2 August 1984): 6–7.

Philosophy Without Principles. *Critical Inquiry* 11 (March 1985): 132–138. Also in *Against Theory*, ed. W. J. T. Mitchell, 132–138. Chicago: University of Chicago Press, 1985.

The Humanities: Asking Better Questions, Doing More Things. Interview. *Federation Review* 8 (March/April 1985): 15–19.

Feeling His Way. Review of The War Diaries of Jean-Paul Sartre: November 1939–March 1940. *The New Republic* (15 April 1985): 32–34.

Le Cosmopolitanisme sans Emancipation: Reponse a Jean-Francois Lyotard. *Critique* (May 1985): 569–580, 584. ORT.

Review of Traditional and Analytical Philosophy: Lectures on the Philosophy of Language, by Ernst Tugendhat. *Journal of Philosophy* 82 (1985): 720–729.

Comments on Sleeper and Edel. *Transactions of The Charles S. Peirce Society* 21 (Winter 1985): 40–48.

Texts and Lumps. *New Literary History* 17 (1985): 1–15. ORT.

Absolutely Non-Absolute. Review of *Philosophical Papers*, by Charles Taylor. *Times Literary Supplement* (6 December 1985): 1379–1380.

The Contingency of Language. *London Review of Books* (17 April 1986): 3–6.

The Contingency of Selfhood. *London Review of Books* (8 May 1986): 11–14.

Sex and the Single Thinker. Review of Sexual Desire: A Moral Philosophy of the Erotic, by Roger Scruton. *The New Republic* (2 June 1986): 34–37.

The Contingency of Community. *London Review of Books* (24 July 1986): 10–14.

Freud and Moral Reflection. In *Pragmatism's Freud: The Moral Disposition of Psychoanalysis*, eds. J. H. Smith and W. Kerrigan, 1–27. Baltimore: Johns Hopkins University Press, 1986. EHO.

Should Hume Be Answered or Bypassed? In *Human Nature and Natural Knowledge: Essays Presented to Marjorie Grene*, ed. A. Donegan, 341–352. Dordrecht: D. Reidel, 1986.

From Logic to Language to Play. *Proceedings and Addresses of the American Philosophical Association* 59 (1986): 747–753.

The Higher Nominalism in a Nutshell, A Reply to Henry Staten. *Critical Inquiry* 12 (1986): 462–466.

On Ethnocentrism: A Reply to Clifford Geertz. *Michigan Quarterly Review* 25 (1986): 525–534. ORT.

Pragmatism, Davidson and Truth. In *Truth and Interpretation: Perspectives on the Philosophy of Donald Davidson*, ed. E. LePore, 333–368. Oxford: Blackwell, 1986. ORT.

Foucault and Epistemology. In *Foucault: A Critical Reader*, ed. D. C. Hoy, 41–49. Oxford: Blackwell, 1986.

Comments on Toulmin's "Conceptual Communities and Rational Conversation." *Archivio di Filosofia* (1986): 189–193.

Beyond Realism and Anti-Realism. In *Wo steht die Analytische Philosophie heute?* ed. L. Nagl and R. Heinrich, 103–115. Vienna: R. Oldenbourg Verlag, Munich, 1986. EHO.

Introduction. In *John Dewey: The Later Works*. Vol. 8, *1933*, ed. J. A. Boydston, ix–xviii. Carbondale: Southern Illinois University Press, 1986.

Interview with Richard Rorty. Interview. *Journal of Literary Studies/ Tydskrif Vir Literatuurwetenskap* 2 (November 1986): 9–13.

Philosophie als Wissenschaft, als Metaphor, und als Politik. In *Die Krise der Phaenomenologie und die Pragmatik des Wissenschaftsfortschritt*, eds. M. Benedikt and R. Burger, 138–149. Vienna: Verlag der Oesterreichischen Staatsdruckerei, 1986.

Non-Reductive Physicalism. In *Theorie der Subjektivitaet*, eds. K. Cramer, et al., 278–296. Frankfurt am Main: Suhrkamp, 1987. ORT.

Posties. Review of Der Philosophische Diskurs der Moderne, by Jürgen Habermas. *London Review of Books* (3 September 1987): 11–12.

Nominalismo e Contestualismo. *Alfabeta* 9 (September 1987): 11–12.

Thugs and Theorists: A Reply to Bernstein. *Political Theory* 15 (November 1987): 564–580.

Unfamiliar Noises: Hesse and Davidson on Metaphor. *Proceedings of the Aristotelian Society Supplement* 61 (1987): 283–296. ORT.

Waren die Gesetze Newtons schon vor Newton Wahr? In *Jahrbuch des Wissenschaftkollegs zu Berlin*. Berlin: Wissenschaftkolleg zu Berlin, 1987.

Science as Solidarity. In *The Rhetoric of the Human Sciences*, eds. J. S. Nelson, A. Megill, and D. N. McCloskey, 38–52. Madison: University of Wisconsin Press, 1987. ORT.

The Priority of Democracy to Philosophy. In *The Virginia Statue of Religious Freedom*, eds. M. Peterson and R. Vaughan, 257–288. Cambridge: Cambridge University Press, 1988. ORT.

Is Natural Science a Natural Kind? In *Construction and Constraint: The Shaping of Scientific Rationality*, ed. E. McMullin, 49–74. Notre Dame, Ind.: Notre Dame University Press, 1988. ORT.

Unger, Castoriadis and the Romance of a National Future. *Northwestern University Law Review* 82 (Winter 1988): 335–351. EHO.

Representation, Social Practice, and Truth. *Philosophical Studies* 54 (1988): 215–228. ORT.

I Professori Sono Meglio dei Torturatori. Interview. *Alpfabeta* 10 (March 1988): 5.

That Old-Time Philosophy. *The New Republic* (4 April 1988): 28–33.

Taking Philosophy Seriously. Review of Heidegger et le Nazisme, by Victor Farias. *The New Republic* (11 April 1988): 31–34.

Review of The Limits of Analysis, by Stanley Rosen. *Independent Journal of Philosophy* 5/6: 153–154.

Two Meanings of "Logocentrism": A Reply to Norris. In *Redrawing the Lines: Analytic Philosophy, Deconstruction and Literary Theory*, ed. Reed Way Dasenbrock, 204–216. Minneapolis: University of Minnesota Press, 1989. EHO.

Identite Morale et Autonomie Privee. In *Michel Foucault Philosophe: Recontre Intenationale*. Paris: Editions du Seuil, 1989: 385–394.

Review of Connections to the World: The Basic Concepts of Philosophy, by Arthur C. Danto, *New York Newsday Books* (March 19, 1989).

Education Without Dogma. *Dissent* (Spring 1989): 198–204.

Is Derrida a Transcendental Philosopher? *Yale Journal of Criticism* (April 1989). EHO.

Social Construction and Composition Theory: A Conversation with Richard Rorty. *Journal of Advanced Composition* 9 (1989): 1–9.

Philosophy and Post-Modernism. *The Cambridge Review* 110 (June 1989): 51–53.

Comments on Castoriadis "The End of Philosophy." *Salmagundi* 82–83 (Spring/Summer 1989): 24–30.

Review of Interpreting Across Boundaries. Ed. E. Deutsch. *Philosophy East and West* (July 1989): 332–337.

Wittgenstein e Heidegger: due percorsi incrociati. *Lettere Intenazionale* 22 (Ottobre/Dicembre 1989): 21–26. In English in *The Cambridge Guide to Heidegger*, ed. C. Guignon. Cambridge: Cambridge University Press, 1993. EHO.

The Humanistic Intellectual: Eleven Theses. *ACLS Occasional Papers* 11 (November 1989).

Philosophy as Science, as Metaphor and as Politics. In *The Institution of Philosophy*, ed. A. Cohen and M. Dascal, 13–33. La Salle, Ill.: Open Court, 1989. EHO.

The Dangers of Over-Philosophication—Reply to Arcilla and Nicholson. *Educational Theory* 40 (1990): 41–44.

Two Cheers for the Cultural Left. *South Atlantic Quarterly* 89 (1990): 227–234.

Another Possible World. *London Review of Books* (8 February 1990): 21. Reprinted in *Martin Heidegger: Politics Art and Technology*, ed. C. Jamme and K. Harries, 34–40. New York and London: Holmes and Meier, 1994; and in translation in the German edition of that book. München: Fink Verlag, 1992.

Truth and Freedom: A Reply to Thomas McCarthy. *Critical Inquiry* 16 (Spring 1990): 633–643.

Foucault/Dewey/Nietzsche. *Raritan* 4 (Spring 1990): 1–8.

Consciousness, Intentionality and Pragmatism. In *Modelos de la Mente*, ed. J. Quiros. Madrid: 1990.

The Philosopher and the Prophet. Review of The Genealogy of Pragmatism, by Cornel West. *Transition* 52 (1991): 70–78.

The Guru of Prague. Review of three books by Jan Patocka. *The New Republic* (1 July 1991): 35–40.

Pragmatismo. In *Dicionario do Pensiamento Contemporanaio*, ed. M. M. Carrilho, 265–278. Lisbon: Publicacoes Dom Quixote, 1991.

Nietzsche, Socrates and Pragmatism. *South African Journal of Philosophy* 10 (August 1991): 61–63.

Intellectuals in Politics. *Dissent* (Autumn 1991).

Comments on Taylor's "Paralectics." In *On the Other: Dialogue and/or Dialectics*, ed. R. P. Scharlemann. Working paper #5 of the UVa Commitee on the Comparative Study of the Individual and Society, 1991: 71–78.

Blunder around for a While. A review of Daniel Dennett's Consciousness Explained. *London Review of Books* (21 November 1991): 3–6.
The Banality of Pragmatism and the Poetry of Justice. In *Pragmatism in Law and Society*, eds. M. Brint and W. Weaver, 89–97. Boulder, Colo.: Westview Press, 1991.
Nietzsche: un philosophe pragmatique. In *Magazine Litteraire* (April 1992): 28–32.
The Intellectuals at the End of Socialism. *The Yale Review* 80 (April 1992): 1–16. An abbreviated version of this article appeared under the title For a More Banal Politics. *Harper's* (May 1992): 16–21.
Introduction to Vladimir Nabokov, *Pale Fire*. London and New York: Everyman's Library, 1992: v–xxiii.
The Pragmatist's Progress. In *Interpretation and Overintepretation* by Umberto Eco et al. Cambridge: Cambridge University Press, 1992: 89–108.
Reply to Andrew Ross. *Dissent* (Spring 1992): 265–267.
What Can You Expect from Anti-Foundationalist Philosophers?: A Reply to Lynn Baker. *Virginia Law Review* 78 (April 1992): 719–727.
Love and Money. *Common Knowledge* 1 (Spring 1992): 12–16.
We Anti-Representationalists. Review of Ideology: An Introduction, by Terry Eagleton. *Radical Philosophy* 60 (Spring 1992): 40–42.
The Feminist Saving Remnant. Review of The Rise and Fall of the American Left, by John Patrick Diggins. *The New Leader* (June 1992): 9–10.
A Pragmatist View of Rationality and Cultural Differences. *Philosophy East and West* 4 (October 1992): 581–596.
Robustness: A Reply to Jean Bethke Elshtain. In *The Politics of Irony*, ed. D. W. Conway and J. E. Seery, 219–223. New York: St. Martin's Press, 1992.
Trotsky and the Wild Orchids. *Common Knowledge* 3 (1992): 140–153. Also in *Wild Orchids and Trotsky: Messages from American Universities*. Ed. M. Edmundson. New York: Viking, 1993.
Reponses de Richard Rorty. To Jacques Bouveresse, Vincent Descombes, Thomas MacCarthy, Alexander Nehamas, and Hilary Putnam. In *Lire Rorty*, ed. J.-P. Cometti, 147–250. Paris: Editions de l'Eclat, 1992.
Dewey entre Hegel et Darwin. *Rue Descartes* 5/6 (Novembre 1992): 53–71.
The Politicization of the Humanities. *UVa Alumni Journal* (Winter 1992).
Interview: On Democracy, Liberalism and the Post-Communist Challenge. *Mesotes: Zeitschrift für philosophischen Ost–West Dialog* 4 (1992): 491–500.
Centers of Moral Gravity: Comments on Donald Spence's "The Hermeneutic Turn." *Psychoanalytic Dialogues* 1 (1993): 21–28.
Holism, Intentionality, and the Ambition of Transcendence. In *Dennett and his Critics: Demystifying Mind*, ed. Bo Dahlbom, 184–202. Oxford: Blackwell, 1993.

Feminism, Ideology and Deconstruction: A Pragmatist View. *Hypatia* 8 (Spring 1993): 96–103.

An Antirepresentationalist View: Comments on Richard Miller, van Fraassen/Sigman, and Churchland and A Comment on Robert Scholes' "Tlon and Truth." In *Realism and Representation*, ed. G. Levine, 125–133, 186–189. Madison: University of Wisconsin Press, 1993.

Review of Ideals and Illusions: On Reconstruction and Deconstruction in Contemporary Critical Theory, by Thomas McCarthy. *Journal of Philosophy* 90 (July 1993): 370–373.

Interview: Intersubjectividad y libertad. Theoria. *Revista de Filosofia* 1 (July 1993): 113–122.

Putnam and the Relativist Menace. *Journal of Philosophy* 90 (September 1993): 443–461.

Interview: Du Pragmatisme en Politique. *Le Banquet* 3 (2eme Semestre 1993): 135–147.

Human Rights, Rationality and Sentimentality. In *On Human Rights: The 1993 Oxford Amnesty Lectures*, eds. S. Hurley and S. Shute, 112–134. New York: Basic Books, 1993. A shortened version, without the footnotes, appeared in *The Yale Review* 4 (October 1993): 1–20.

Paroxysms and Politics. Review of The Passion of Michel Foucault, by James Miller. *Salmagundi* 97 (Winter 1993): 61–68.

Replies to Burzta and Buchowski, Dziemidok, Gierszewski, Kmita, Kwiek, Morawski, Szahaj, Zeidler, and Zeidler-Janiszewska. *Ruch Filozoficzny* 2 (1994): 178–179, 183–184, 188–189, 194–195, 198–200, 205–207, 209–210, 214–216, 218.

Review of Willful Liberalism: Voluntarism and Individuality in Political Theory and Practice, by Richard Flathman. *Political Theory* 1 (February 1994): 190–194.

The Unpatriotic Academy. *New York Times*, February 13, 1994, op-ed page.

Why Can't a Man Be More Like a Woman, and Other Problems in Moral Philosophy. Review of Moral Prejudices: Essays in Ethics, by Annette Baier. *London Review of Books* 4 (24 February 1994): 3–6.

Taylor on Self-Celebration and Gratitude. *Philosophy and Phenomenological Research* 1 (March 1994): 197–201.

Does Democracy Need Foundations? In *Politisches Denken: Jahrbuch 1993*, eds. Volker Gerhardt et al., 21–23. Stuttgart & Weimar: Metzler Verlag, 1994.

Review of The Grandeur and Twilight of Radical Universalism, by Agnes Heller and Ferenc Feher. *Thesis Eleven* 37 (1994): 119–126.

Religion as Conversation-Stopper. *Common Knowledge* 1 (Spring 1994): 1–6.

Tales of Two Disciplines. *Callaloo* 2 (1994): 575–607.

Dewey between Hegel and Darwin. In *Modernist Impulses in the Human Sciences*, ed. D. Ross. Baltimore: Johns Hopkins University Press, 1994.

Sex, Lies, and Virginia's Voters. *New York Times*, October 13, 1994, op-ed page.

A Leg-Up for Oliver North. Review of Dictatorship of Virtue: Multiculturalism and the Battle for America's Future, by Richard Bernstein. *London Review of Books* (20 October 1994): 13–14. A revised version appeared in *Harper's*, January 1995, under the title Demonizing the Academy.

Taylor on Truth. In *Philosophy in an Age of Pluralism: The Philosophy of Charles Taylor in Question*, ed. J. Tully, 20–36. Cambridge: Cambridge University Press, 1994.

Does Academic Freedom Have Philosophical Presuppositions? *Academe* 6 (November/December 1994): 52–63.

Sind Aussagen universelle Geltungsansprüche? *Deutsche Zeitschrift für Philosophie* 6 (1994): 975–988.

Two Cheers for Elitism. Review of The Revolt of the Elites and the Betrayal of Democracy, by Christopher Lasch. *The New Yorker*, January 30, 1995: 86–89.

Is Derrida a Quasi-Transcendental Philosopher? Review of *Jacques Derrida*, by Geoffrey Bennington and Jacques Derrida. Chicago: University of Chicago Press, 1993, *Contemporary Literature* 36 (Spring 1995): 173–200.

Response to Steven Lukes. *Dissent* (Spring 1995): 264–265.

Toward a Post-Metaphysical Culture. Interview. *The Harvard Journal of Philosophy* (Spring 1995): 58–66.

The End of Leninism and History as Comic Frame. In *History and the Idea of Progress*, eds. A. M. Melzer et al., 211–226. Ithaca, N.Y.: Cornell University Press, 1995.

Untruth and Consequences. Review of Killing Time, by Paul Feyerabend. *The New Republic* (31 July 1995): 32–36.

Contributions to *Rorty and the Pragmatists*. Ed. H. Saatkamp. Nashville: Vanderbilt University Press, 1995; Response to Hartshorne: 29–36; Response to Lavine: 50–53; Response to Bernstein: 68–71; Response to Gouinlock: 91–99; Response to Hance: 122–125; Response to Haack: 148–153; Response to Farrell: 189–196; Philosophy and the Future: 197–205.

Is Truth a Goal of Inquiry?: Davidson vs. Wright. *Philosophical Quarterly* 180 (July 1995): 281–300.

Cranes and Skyhooks. Review of Darwin's Dangerous Idea: Evolution and the Meanings of Life, by Daniel Dennett. *Lingua Franca* (August 1995): 62–66.

Introduction to reprint of *John Dewey: An Intellectual Portrait*, by Sidney Hook. Buffalo: Prometheus, 1995: xi–xviii.

Deconstruction. In *The Cambridge History of Literary Criticism*. Vol. 8, *From Formalism to Poststructuralism*, ed. R. Selden, 166–196. Cambridge: Cambridge University Press, 1995.

Color-Blind in the Marketplace. Review of The End of Racism: Principles for a Multicultural Society, by Dinesh d'Souza. *New York Times Book Review* (24 September 1995): 9.

Consolation Prize. Review of The Unconsoled, by Kazuo Ishiguro. *Village Voice Literary Supplement* 139 (October 1995): 13.

Campaigns and Movements. *Dissent* (Winter 1995): 55–60.

A Spectre is Haunting the Intellectuals. Review of Spectres of Marx, by Jaques Derrida. *European Journal of Philosophy* 3 (December 1995): 289–298.

Habermas, Derrida and the Functions of Philosophy. *Revue Internationale de Philosophie* 4 (1995): 437–460.

»» ««

Index

»» ««

About the Contributors

JÜRGEN HABERMAS is Professor Emeritus, Philosophische Fakultät, Johann Wolfgang Goethe-Universität, Frankfurt.

RICHARD RORTY is University Professor of Humanities, the University of Virginia.

LESZEK KOLAKOWSKI is a Fellow of All Souls College, Oxford.

ERNEST GELLNER was Professor of Social Anthropology at Cambridge University.

JÓZEF NIZNIK is Professor, Institute of Philosophy and Sociology, Polish Academy of Sciences.

JOHN T. SANDERS is Visiting Professor, Graduate School for Social Research, Institute of Philosophy and Sociology, Polish Academy of Sciences, and Professor, Department of Philosophy, Rochester Institute of Technology.

MAREK BIELECKI is Assistant Professor, Department of Philosophy, University of Warsaw and the California State University at Hayward.

ADAM CHMIELEWSKI is Assistant Professor, Department of Philosophy, University of Wroclaw.

PIOTR GUTOWSKI is Assistant Professor, Department of Philosophy, Catholic University of Lublin.

ANDRZEJ GRZEGORCZYK is Professor Emeritus, Institute of Philosophy and Sociology, Polish Academy of Sciences.

JÓZEF KOSIAN is Professor, Department of Philosophy, University of Wroclaw.

WLADYSLAW KRAJEWSKI is Professor Emeritus, Department of Philosophy, University of Warsaw.

LESZEK KUZNICKI is Professor and President of the Polish Academy of Sciences.

STEFAN MORAWSKI is Professor Emeritus, Department of Philosophy, University of Warsaw.

DÉSIRÉE PARK is Professor, Department of Philosophy, Concordia University (Canada).

MAREK J. SIEMEK is Professor, Department of Philosophy, University of Warsaw.

GRAZYNA SKAPSKA is Professor, Department of Sociology, Jagiellonian University, Cracow.

ANDRZEJ SZAHAJ is Assistant Professor, Department of Philosophy, University of Torun.

ANDRZEJ WALICKI is Professor, Department of Philosophy, University of Notre Dame, U.S.

RAFAL WIERZCHOSLAWSKI is Instructor, Department of Philosophy, Catholic University of Lublin.

ISBN 0-275-95715-2
90000>
EAN
9 780275 957155
HARDCOVER BAR CODE